Alaska Ports
of Call 1999

Swift Recovery.
& Happy Cruising
Gord.

Len & Pauline
March/00

Excerpted from Fodor's *The Best Cruises '99*

Fodor's Travel Publications, Inc.
New York • Toronto • London • Sydney • Auckland
www.fodors.com

Fodor's Alaska Ports of Call

EDITOR: M. T. Schwartzman

Editorial Contributors: Wendy Determan, Don Pitcher, Heidi Sarna
Editorial Production: Linda K. Schmidt
Maps: David Lindroth, *cartographer*; Robert Blake, *map editor*
Design: Fabrizio La Rocca, *creative director*; Guido Caroti, *associate art director*; Jolie Novak, *photo editor*
Production/Manufacturing: Robert B. Shields
Technical Illustration: Christopher A. Wilson
Cover Photograph: Pat O'Hara/Tony Stone
Cover Design: Allison Saltzman

Copyright

ISBN 0–679–00172–7

Special Sales

Fodor's Travel Publications are available at special discounts for bulk purchases for sales promotions or premiums. Special editions, including personalized covers, excerpts of existing guides, and corporate imprints, can be created in large quantities for special needs. For more information, contact your local bookseller or write to Special Markets, Fodor's Travel Publications, 201 East 50th Street, New York, NY 10022. Inquiries from Canada should be directed to your local Canadian bookseller or sent to Random House of Canada, Ltd., Marketing Department, 2775 Matheson Boulevard East, Mississauga, Ontario L4W 4P7. Inquiries from the United Kingdom should be sent to Fodor's Travel Publications, 20 Vauxhall Bridge Road, London SW1V 2SA, England.

PRINTED IN THE UNITED STATES OF AMERICA
10 9 8 7 6 5 4 3 2 1

CONTENTS

3   The Alaska Cruise Fleet   *109*

4   Itineraries   *124*

Index   *129*

Maps

Don't Forget to Write

You can use this book in the confidence that all prices and opening times are based on information supplied to us at press time; Fodor's cannot accept responsibility for any errors. Time inevitably brings changes, so always confirm information when it matters—especially if you're making a detour to visit a specific place.

For ongoing updates of the most intriguing cruise itineraries, candid reviews of new vessels, and links to the best cruise sites, visit the Cruise News section of Fodor's Web site, www.fodors.com/cruise.

Were the restaurants we recommended as described? Did you find a museum we recommended a waste of time? Keeping a travel guide fresh and up-to-date is a big job, and we welcome your feedback, positive *and* negative. If you have complaints, we'll look into them and revise our entries when the facts warrant it. If you've discovered a special place that we haven't included, we'll pass the information along to our correspondents and have them check it out. So send us your thoughts via e-mail at editors@fodors.com (specifying the name of the book on the subject line) or on paper in care of the Alaska Ports of Call editor at Fodors, 201 East 50th Street, New York, New York 10022. In the meantime, have a wonderful trip!

Karen Cure
Editorial Director

THE CHARACTER OF ALASKA

WHEN I TOOK my first cruise to Alaska, I was drawn by the imagery, bigger than life, associated with the 49th American state. After all, it's called "The Great Land," a loose translation of the Aleut word "Alyeska." Alaska boasts the highest mountain in North America—Denali, "The High One" in the Athabascan tongue—as well as 17 of the 20 highest peaks in the United States. There are more bald eagles here than anywhere else. More totem poles. Thousands of glaciers. King-size salmon and humongous halibut.

There is nothing ordinary about this land—or the people who call it home. The "Last Frontier" demands self-sufficiency, ingenuity, and bravery. The people of Alaska embody an egalitarian spirit, adventurous and independent. This is the character of Alaska. Status in Alaska is measured by longevity. Newcomers are called cheechakos. Old-timers are known as sourdoughs. But the greatest honor is reserved for the pioneers, those who have spent the most time in the country—at least 30 years.

I have a great affinity for Alaska and its people, even though I live far across the continent, outside New York City, where our mountains are skyscrapers and wildlife means mostly pigeons. My home is not much of a frontier, but deep inside me—as in, I suspect, so many Americans—there is a need for space. Room to roam is something Alaska has in abundance. As the largest state in the Union, its 586,412 square miles equal one-fifth the land mass of the Lower 48. A popular postcard shows Alaska superimposed on a map of the United States: It stretches nearly from sea to shining sea. (Look for this postcard in souvenir shops.)

Today's Alaskan combines tenacity and technology to live in a land that remains challenging. Like the towering mountains and jutting fjords that line the Inside Passage, the Alaskan character has been shaped by the elements. All of southeast Alaska lies in a rain forest (Ketchikan receives more than 150 inches of rain a year), and except for Haines and Skagway in the north, there are no roads linking the towns along the Panhandle. In fact, Juneau is the only state capital in the United States that cannot be reached over land. You fly in or you sail in, but you don't drive in.

Geography alone makes Alaska an ideal cruise destination. On a typical seven-day itinerary, you'll visit up to four ports of call and one or two scenic bays or fjords. And the nature of ship travel is perfectly suited to discovering what Alaska is all about. From the deck of a cruise ship, you can come face to face with a glacier. From the dining room, you can watch a full moon rise over a snow-striped mountain. And you can enjoy it all in the lap of luxury.

The natural beauty of Alaska is hard to overstate. As you prepare for your cruise, consider these facts about Alaska's grandeur:

• The Inside Passage, the traditional route north to Alaska and a favorite among cruise passengers, stretches 1,000 miles from Puget Sound, Washington, in the south to Skagway, Alaska, in the north. From there, the Gulf of Alaska arcs for another 500 miles from east to west.

• Alaska has thousands of glaciers. No one really knows how many, but estimates range from 5,000 to 100,000. Among the most famous ones that cruise passengers visit are LeConte outside Petersburg, the southernmost calving glacier in North America, and Hubbard at Yakutat Bay in the Gulf of Alaska, 6 miles wide and 76 miles long to its source. There are 12 tidewater glaciers in Glacier Bay National Park and Preserve and another 16 glaciers in College Fjord off Prince William Sound. The Malaspina Glacier, at the entrance to Yakutat Bay, is bigger than the state of Rhode Island.

• Tongass National Forest, which spans great stretches of the Inside Passage, is the largest national forest in the United States. Wrangell-St. Elias National Park, a UNESCO World Heritage Site east of Anchorage and bordering the Gulf of Alaska, is the largest national park in the United States—six times the size of Yellowstone.

In such broad expanses of land, airplanes have become as common as taxis in New York. The bush plane in particular holds a special place in Alaska folklore: This was the machine that opened the wilderness and that, to this day, provides the only access to remote communities. In South Anchorage, a suburb just beyond downtown, propeller planes are parked one after another like the family car. Lake Hood, near the airport, is the world's largest and busiest seaplane base; if you have time, be sure to stop by to watch the brightly painted Cessnas and Dehavilland Beavers coming and going hourly. Anchorage pays special tribute to the bush pilots of the past. Two museums, the Alaska Aviation Heritage Museum and the Reeve Aviation Picture Museum, are dedicated to their exploits. Even today, the bush pilot is a revered figure, and I can think of few better ways to appreciate the character of the people and the wonder of the land than from the window of a Cessna.

MERE NUMBERS, however, cannot capture the effect of Alaska on the human spirit. Before I went to Alaska, never had I seen somebody catch their breath. Yet this was the genuine reaction of my traveling companion as she saw her first glacier—the mighty Mendenhall, its icy face peeking out from a veil of mist just 13 miles from downtown Juneau. While driving back to the pier, we passed Salmon Creek, where the annual salmon run was in full swing. The water was so thick with fish, we could have waded in and plucked one out.

Wildlife is everywhere in Alaska. The state has 15 species of whales. Southeast Alaska has more brown bears than the rest of the United States combined. Alaska ranks number one in bald eagles (Florida is number two).

On my second cruise to Alaska, our small ship happened upon a couple of sleeping whales, their blue-black bodies barely breaking the surface of the water. The captain cut the engines (so we wouldn't disturb the whales' slumber), and for a good while we just observed their breathing. Later the whole scene was replayed in the main lounge on videotape.

Not long after, we experienced another Kodak moment: a brown bear foraging on the shoreline. Again, the captain held our position as the bear wandered along the water's edge. When the bear was done, he moved on, as did we. The captain, however, had one more treat in store for us. At a rushing waterfall, he nudged the bow of our small-ship under the gush of water. Raincoat-clad crew members filled pitchers with glacial runoff, and soon we all enjoyed a refreshment of cool mineral water. Such are the simple pleasures of an Alaskan cruise: calving glaciers, sea lions and seals, and sensational sunsets—at midnight.

Bird-watchers will have a field day looking for bald eagles. These birds have long represented courage and power, so it is appropriate that so many bald eagles populate Alaska. In fact, eagles are so numerous you'll have to remind yourself that they remain a threatened species. There's even an eagle hospital, the Alaska Raptor Rehabilitation Center in Sitka, where eagles and other birds of prey are nursed back to health. You can visit the center if your ship calls in Ketchikan. If not, bald eagles are easily spotted in the wild: Look for their bright white heads perched high in the tree tops—or telephone poles—all along the Inside Passage.

In addition to glaciers and wildlife, there's an exciting frontier history to discover. You will be just the latest in a long line of visitors who have come over the ages. Scientists estimate that the first people arrived in Alaska some 15,000 years ago, when they migrated across the Bering Land Bridge from Asia. (Some expedition ships sail from Alaska to the Russian Far East, allowing you to follow the migration pattern in reverse.) The earliest evidence of human habitation along the Inside Passage can be found in Wrangell, where petroglyphs—mysterious markings carved into rocks and boulders on the beach—are thought to be at least 8,000 years old.

Alaska's indigenous people belong to one of four groups: Aleuts, Athabascans, Eskimos, and Northwest Coast Indians. The Aleuts live on the Aleutian Islands. Athabascans populate the Interior, while Eskimos inhabit the Arctic regions of the Far North. The native Alaskans you are most likely to meet during your cruise are the Tlingit, Haida, or Tsimshian Indians of the Inside Passage.

The Tlingit are responsible for Alaska's famous totem carvings. Totem poles tell the story of a great event, identify members of the same clan, and honor great leaders. The best place to see totem poles is Saxman Native Village in Ketchikan, where you'll find my favorite—the Abraham Lincoln totem pole, with an image of Honest Abe at its top. Don't miss the collection of original totems at the Totem Heritage Center. These are the oldest authentic poles in Alaska, some dating back about 200 years. Today, you can still see Native artisans at work in Ketchikan, Haines, and Sitka, where the totem poles are lesser known but equally impressive.

Northwest Coast Indians are noted for their many artistic skills; totem carvings are just the most celebrated example. Miniature totem reproductions are among the most popular souvenirs in Alaska, but ceremonial masks, decorative paddles, and woven baskets also make great gifts. These and other native crafts are sold throughout the Inside Passage. Before you buy, look for the Silver Hand label, which guarantees authenticity. (For nonnative items, check for the "Made in Alaska" polar bear logo.)

CRAFTS ARE JUST ONE way for cruise passengers to appreciate the local culture. Native Alaskans are often happy to show you around. In Juneau, Ketchikan, and Sitka, you can book a sightseeing tour with a native point of view. Performances of native dance and traditional storytelling entertain visitors in Juneau, Sitka, and Haines. Ask about these aboard your ship or at the visitor information office near the pier.

In the footsteps of native Alaskans came European explorers. The first was Vitus Bering, who "discovered" Alaska and claimed it for Russia in 1741. The Russians made Kodiak their capital, before moving the colonial seat of government to Sitka in 1808. The faithful still worship in the onion-domed Russian Orthodox Church, one of southeast Alaska's most recognizable landmarks. Next came British and Spanish explorers. Cook Inlet in Anchorage is named for Captain Cook; a statue of him dominates Resolution Park, a terraced lookout perched atop the inlet that bears his name. One member of Cook's expedition was George Vancouver, namesake of the Canadian port city where most Alaska cruises begin or end. Ketchikan sits on an island named after a Spaniard, the Count of Revillagigedo, viceroy of New Spain and a proponent of Spanish exploration of Alaska. Wrangell Island, at the southern end of the Inside Passage, is the only Alaskan port of call to have flown three flags—Russian, British, and finally American.

The connection with Europe is echoed in the nicknames given to some of Alaska's port cities. Valdez is often referred to as Alaska's "Little Switzerland" for the mountains that ring the city. Petersburg is Alaska's "Little Norway," and the town's residents still celebrate their Scandinavian heritage every May in a festival of Norwegian song and dance. If you are lucky enough to visit Petersburg on your cruise (only the smallest ships and ferries call here), you may be treated to a performance at the Sons of Norway Hall—followed by a Norwegian smorgasbord.

ALASKA HAS a reputation for ruggedness—both in the land and in its people. As for the latter, the rough-and-tumble character of Alaska's past is best sensed in Ketchikan. Perhaps this has something to do with the city's history, filled with tall tales of miners, loggers, and fisherman. You can still walk the boardwalk along Creek Street, "where men and fish went upstream to spawn," and see Dolly's House, now a museum but once a brothel—one of many that lined the town's notorious red-light district.

Things are more serene these days, and many Alaskans are given to more spiritual pursuits—like painting. John Webber, a British artist, accompanied Captain Cook to Alaska in 1778. In 1903, Brooklyn-born Sydney Laurence came to Alaska and stayed until 1940, painting grand depictions of the local landscape. You can see the renderings of Webber, Laurence, and others in the Anchorage Museum of History and Art. Contemporary artists prefer Homer and Haines; both have established reputations as artists' communities. Galleries that feature the work of local artists are common in all port cities. Seek them out—a portrait of Alaska is one of the best keepsakes.

Perhaps the most colorful episode in Alaska's storied history was the Gold Rush, which reached a fever pitch during the winter of 1897–98. It's ironic to think how William Seward purchased Alaska from Russia for $7.2 million, only to be publicly ridiculed for his "folly." But when word got out that gold had been discovered in the Far North, the news set off a stampede of legendary proportion. Some say up to 100,000 men headed for the gold fields. More conservative estimates put the number as low as 30,000. In either case, the Klondike Gold Rush put Alaska on the map, as gold-crazed prospectors, con-men, and assorted other characters clamored up the Inside Passage.

The Gold Rush has held a lifelong fascination for me. As a child, I first read Jack London's accounts of the heady Gold Rush days, and I still have my original color-illustrated copy of *Call of the Wild*. This classic novel, based on London's personal experiences, is required reading for anyone cruising

Alaska. Also be sure to see the Walt Disney's adaptation of London's *White Fang*; it was filmed on location in Haines.

If, like me, you're an aficionado of Gold-Rush history, choose a cruise that includes a call at Skagway, the gateway to the Klondike a century ago. As you sail the Lynn Canal, the natural channel that connects Skagway with the rest of the Inside Passage, keep in mind that you are following the same route and traveling in the same manner (albeit a bit more luxurious) as the original prospectors. Once ashore, you'll hear the story of Frank Reid (the good guy) and Jefferson Randolph "Soapy" Smith (the bad guy), who shot it out for control of Skagway. You'll hear how superintendent Samuel Steele of the Canadian Mounted Police called Skagway "the roughest place on earth." And you'll learn how, after the Gold Rush died down, Skagway became the birthplace of Alaska's tourism industry.

TODAY, the town looks much as it did in the early 1900s. The entire downtown area is a National Historic District, part of Klondike Gold Rush National Historic Park. The yellow 1930s touring limousines you see are operated by the Skagway Streetcar Company, which re-creates Martin Itjen's original Skagway sightseeing tour. This is a very popular shore excursion, as is a ride on the vintage parlor cars of the White Pass and Yukon Railway. It's one of the few chances cruise passengers have to venture deep into the mountains—just as prospectors traveled over the treacherous White Pass. From the cars of the train, you can still see the "Trail of '98," a footpath worn permanently into the mountainside.

Few establishments evoke the spirit of the frontier like the local saloon, and as a cruise passenger you'll have the opportunity to visit two of Alaska's most famous (depending on your itinerary). Near the cruise ship docks in Skagway is the Red Onion Saloon—one of my favorite places in Alaska. To step inside is to return to 1898, when the saloon was founded; the bartender still serves drinks on the original mahogany bar. In Juneau, another Gold-Rush town, the Red Dog Saloon has been a favorite local watering hole since early this century. In fact, Wyatt Earp's six-shooter still hangs on wall. It's said he left it here while just passing through.

Like Wyatt Earp, you too will just be passing through. But, as you are about to discover, cruising is a great way to see "The Great Land." I encourage you to spend as much time as you can in Alaska. Bring plenty of film or videotape, don't forget a rain slicker, and to try everything. Go hiking, fishing, flightseeing. Ride the railroads, book a salmon bake, scope for eagles. Think big—and be sure to buy a souvenir totem pole.

— M.T. Schwartzman
Editor, *Alaska Ports of Call 1999*

1 Cruise Primer

CHOOSING YOUR CRUISE

The right ship is one that makes you comfortable. Every ship has its own personality, depending on whether it was designed for ocean cruising, coastal cruising, or expedition cruising. Big ships are more stable and offer a huge variety of activities and facilities. Smaller ships feel intimate, like private clubs. Each type of ship satisfies a certain type of passenger, and for every big-ship fan there is somebody who would never set foot aboard one of these "floating resorts."

Comparing Ships

In order to compare cruise ships, you need to speak "ship talk." Vessels are generally described according to their passenger capacity, gross registered tonnage, passenger-to-crew ratio, and space ratio. A ship's passenger capacity is usually based on double occupancy, meaning the normal cruise complement of the vessel with two passengers in each cabin. This does not include third or fourth passengers in a cabin, which on some ships can greatly increase the total passenger count. Gross registered tonnage is commonly used to measure a vessel's size. Technically, it is a measurement of the ship's volume, with 1 gross registered ton equal to 100 cubic ft. Passenger-to-crew ratio indicates the number of passengers served by each crew member—the lower the ratio, the better the level of service. Space ratio, the ship's tonnage divided by its passenger capacity, allows you to compare a ship's roominess. The higher the ratio, the more spacious a vessel will feel. The roomiest ships have ratios of 40:1 or better; ships with ratios of less than 28:1 may feel cramped.

But when choosing your cruise, the size of the ship isn't the only factor to consider. You also need to find out about the nature of the experience you will have—the lifestyle and activities available by day and after dark, the mealtime hours and dining-room dress codes, how roomy the ship is, and how good the service is apt to be. Equally important are your itinerary, the accommodations, and the cost of the cruise.

Types of Ships

Although all ocean liners are equipped with swimming pools, spas, nightclubs, theaters, and casinos, there are three distinct types: classic liners, cruise liners, and megaships. Many **classic liners,** ships constructed between 1950 and 1969 for transatlantic or other ocean crossings, are still sailing in the fleets of a few cruise lines. Beginning in the 1960s, ship lines began to create vessels specifically for cruising. Some of these **cruise liners** were brand new; others were converted ferries or freighters. Vessels known as **megaships,** the biggest cruise ships ever built, first appeared in the late 1980s and, with their immense proportions and passenger capacities, immediately established a new standard of cruise-ship design.

Cruises are also available aboard a number of smaller ships, such as expedition ships and coastal cruisers.

Cruise Liners

When shipbuilders stopped constructing vessels for transportation and started designing them for vacationing, the cruise liner entered the scene. On these ships, outdoor deck space is plentiful; stateroom space is not. Many have a wraparound outdoor promenade deck that allows you to stroll or jog the perimeter of the ship. Older cruise liners resemble the transatlantic ships from which they are descended: Decks are stacked one atop the other in steps, and the hull amidships may appear to droop, so the bow and stern seem to curve upward. In the newest cruise liners, traditional meets trendy. You find atrium lobbies and expansive sun and sports decks, picture windows instead of portholes, and cabins that open onto private verandas. The smallest cruise liners carry 500 passengers and are no bigger than 10,000 tons, while the largest accommodate 1,500 passengers, exceed 50,000 tons, and are stuffed with diversions—almost like megaships.

Megaships

The centerpiece of most megaships is a three-, five-, or seven-story central atrium. However, these giant vessels are most easily recognized by their boxy profile: The hull and superstructure rise straight out of the water, as many as 14 stories tall, topped out by a huge sun or sports deck with a jogging track and swimming pool, which may be Olympic size. Some megaships, but not all, also have a wraparound promenade deck. Like the latest cruise liners, picture windows are standard equipment, and cabins in the top categories have private verandas. From their casinos and discos to their fitness centers, everything is proportionally bigger and more extravagant than on other ships. Between 1,500 and 2,500 passengers can be accommodated, and tonnage ranges from 70,000 to 100,000 or more.

Expedition Ships

Vessels of this type are designed to reach into the most remote corners of the world. Shallow drafts allow them to navigate up rivers, close to coastlines, and into shallow coves. Hulls may be hardened for sailing in Antarctic ice. Motorized rubber landing craft known as Zodiacs, kept on board, make it possible for passengers to put ashore almost anywhere. However, because the emphasis during cruises aboard expedition ships tends to be on learning and exploring, the ships don't have casinos, showrooms, multiple bars and lounges, and other typical ocean-liner diversions. Instead, they have theaters for lectures, well-stocked libraries, and enrichment programs, led by experts, as entertainment. The smallest expedition ships carry fewer than 100 passengers and register just over 2,000 tons. The largest carries nearly 200 people and registers 9,000 tons.

Coastal Cruisers

Closely related to the riverboat is its modern-day equivalent, the coastal cruiser. Designed more for exploring than entertaining, these yachtlike ships are able to sail to remote waterways and ports. Some have forward gangways for bow landings or carry a fleet of Zodiac landing craft. Unlike larger expedition ships, they do not have ice-hardened hulls. Registering no more than 100 tons and carrying only about 100 passengers, coastal cruisers offer few onboard facilities and public spaces—perhaps just a dining room and a multipurpose lounge.

The Cruise Experience

Your cruise experience will be shaped by several factors, and to determine whether a particular ship's style will suit you, you need to do a bit of research. Is a full program of organized activities scheduled by day? What happens in the evening? Are there one or two seatings in the dining room? If there is more than one, you will not be allowed to arrive and exit as the spirit moves you but instead must show up promptly when service begins—and clear out within a specified time. What kind of entertainment is offered after dark? And how often do passengers dress up for dinner? Some cruises are fancier than others.

Although no two cruises are quite the same, even aboard the same ship, the cruise experience tends to fall into three categories.

Formal

Formal cruises embody the ceremony of cruising. Generally available on ocean liners and cruise yachts sailing for seven days or longer, formal cruises recall the days when traveling by ship was an event in itself. By day, shipboard lifestyle is generally unstructured, with few organized activities. Tea and bouillon may be served to the accompaniment of music from a classical trio in the afternoon. Ashore, passengers may be treated to a champagne beach party. Meals in the dining room are served in a single seating, and passengers enjoy the finest cuisine afloat. Jackets and ties for men are the rule for dinner, tuxedos are not uncommon, and the dress code is observed faithfully throughout the evening. Pianists, cabaret acts, and local entertainers provide nighttime diversion. Service is extremely attentive and personalized. Passenger-to-crew and space ratios are best. Because these cruises tend to attract destination-oriented passengers, shore excursions—such as private museum tours—sometimes are included in the fare, as are pre- or post-cruise land packages and sometimes even tips.

Semiformal

Semiformal cruises are a bit more relaxed than their formal counterparts. Meals are served in two seatings on ocean liners or one seating on specialty ships, menu choices are plentiful, and the cuisine is on a par with that available in better restaurants. Men tend to wear a jacket and tie to dinner most nights. Adding a distinct flair to the dining room is the common practice of staffing the restaurant with waiters of one nationality. Featured dishes may be prepared table side, and you often are able, with advance notice, to order a special diet, such as kosher, low-salt, low-cholesterol, sugar free, or vegetarian (*see* Dining *in* On Board, *below*). There is a daily program of scheduled events, but there's time for more independent pursuits; passengers with similar interests are often encouraged to meet at appointed times for chess or checkers, deck games, and other friendly contests. Production-style shows are staged each evening, but the disco scene may not be too lively. Passenger-to-crew and space ratios assure good service and plenty of room for each passenger. Look for semiformal cruises aboard classic liners, cruise liners, and megaships on voyages of seven days or longer.

Casual

Casual cruises are the most popular. Shipboard dress and lifestyle are informal. Meals in the dining room are served in two seatings on ocean liners and one seating on specialty ships; menus are usually not extensive, and the food is good but not extraordinary; your options may be limited if you have special dietetic requirements. Men dress in sport shirts and slacks for dinner most nights, in jackets and ties only two or three evenings of a typical seven-day sailing. Aboard casual ocean liners, activities are more diverse than on formal and semiformal ships, and there is almost always something going on, from bingo to beer-chugging contests. Las Vegas–style variety shows or Broadway revues headline the evening entertainment. Discos bop into the wee hours. Passenger-to-crew and space ratios are generally good, but service tends to be less personal. On the smallest ships, activities on board will be limited as indicated in Types of Ships, *above*.

Look for casual cruises aboard classic liners, cruise liners, and megaships sailing three- to seven-day itineraries to fun-and-sun destinations; motor-sailing ships; and coastal cruisers calling on more unusual ports.

How Long to Sail

After you choose the type of ship and cruise experience you prefer, you must decide on how long to sail: Do you want a two-day cruise to nowhere or a 100-day journey around the world? Two key factors to keep in mind are how much money you want to spend and how experienced are you at cruising—it probably wouldn't be a good idea to circum-navigate the globe your first time at sea.

You may want to try a **weeklong cruise.** For some people, seven days is still too short—just when you learn your way around the ship, it's time to go home. On **10- or 11-day sailings,** you get more ports as well as more time at sea, but you won't pay as much as on **two-week sailings.** Many experienced cruisers feel it's just not worth the effort to board a ship for anything less than 14 days, so they opt for either a single 14-day itinerary or sign up for two seven-day trips back-to-back, taking advantage of the discounts offered by some lines for consecutive sailings.

Ship Itineraries

In choosing the best cruise for you, a ship's itinerary is an-other important factor. The length of the cruise will deter-mine the variety and number of ports you visit, but so will the type of itinerary and the point of departure. Some cruises, known as **loop cruises,** start and end at the same point and usually explore ports close to one another; **one-way cruises** start at one port and end at another and range farther afield.

Note: Cruise itineraries listed in Chapter 4 are for the 1999 Alaska season but are subject to change. Contact your travel agent or the cruise line directly for up-to-the-minute itineraries.

Cost

For one price, a cruise gives you all your meals, accom-modations, and onboard entertainment. The only extras are tips, shore excursions, shopping, bar bills, and other inci-dentals. The axiom "the more you pay, the more you get" doesn't always hold true: While higher fares do prevail for better ships, which have more comfortable cabins, more at-tractive decor, and better service, the passenger in the least-expensive inside cabin eats the same food, sees the same shows, and shares the same amenities as one paying more than $1,000 per day for the top suite on any given ship.

A handy way to compare costs of different ships is to look at the per diem—the price of a cruise on a daily basis per passenger, based on double occupancy. (For instance, the per diem is $100 for a seven-day cruise that costs $700 per person when two people share the same cabin.)

BOOKING YOUR CRUISE

Using a Travel Agent

A good travel agent is the secret to a good cruise. Since nearly all cruises are sold through travel agents, the agent you choose to work with can be just as important as the ship you sail on. So how do you know if an agent or agency is right for you? Talk to friends, family, and colleagues who have used an agency to book a cruise. The most qualified agents are members of CLIA (Cruise Lines International Association). Agents who are CLIA Accredited Cruise Counsellors or Master Cruise Counsellors have had extensive cruise and ship inspection experience. If you opt for a cruise-only agency (*see below*), they should also be a member of NACOA (National Association of Cruise-Only Agencies). These agents are also experienced cruisers. Finally, the most reputable agencies, both full-service and cruise-only, are members of ASTA (American Society of Travel Agents). *Remember, though: The best travel agent puts your needs first.*

The size of a travel agency tends to matter less than the experience of its staff. A good cruise agent will ask you many detailed questions about your past vacations, your lifestyle, and even your friends and your hobbies. Only by getting to know you can an agent successfully match you to a ship and a cruise. Never book a cruise with an agent who asks a few cursory questions before handing you a brochure.

Conversely, think of an agent as your travel consultant. Ask the agent any questions you may have about cruising. Most travel agents who book cruises have cruised extensively, and they can help you to decide on a cruise line and a ship. If you have a problem with the cruise line before, during, or after your cruise, they can act as an intermediary.

Of course, you want the best price. However, it's important not to make price your single greatest concern. Value—what you get for your money—is just as important as the dollar amount you pay. Keep in mind that the advertised prices you see in newspapers are usually for the lowest grade cabin. A better cabin—one with a window and maybe a private veranda—is likely to cost more. However, it pays to be wary of agencies that quote prices that are much higher than advertised. It's a bad sign when an agency's ads are blatant lies to get you in the door.

Perhaps the best way to shop for a cruise is to decide first on a cruise line and ship, and then to shop for an agency. Most agencies have "partnerships" with certain cruise lines, which can work to your advantage. By agreeing to sell a lot of cabins (and therefore, of course, by promoting certain cruise lines) the agency gets a better rate from the cruise line. The agency can then afford to offer a "discounted" price to the public.

When it comes down to it, the very top travel agencies can more or less get you the same price on most cruises, because they'll guarantee that if the cruise line lowers the price in a promotion, you'll get the better deal. Look for an agency that offers this guarantee. Remember, too, that agencies that are willing to go the extra mile for their clients are the best agencies. This means providing free cruise-discount newsletters, cabin upgrades, dollar-stretching advice, and, arguably most important of all, 24-hour service in case of a problem are your best bet.

Cruise-Only Travel Agents

As the name implies, "cruise-only" travel agencies specialize in selling cruises. However, these agencies can sell you air tickets and other travel arrangements, too, as part of your cruise package. Sometimes, your choice may be limited to a package put together by the cruise line. Increasingly, though, cruise-only agencies are putting together their own custom-designed cruise vacations. Because they sell only cruises—and because they sell so many cruises—cruise-only agencies can generally get you the best deal.

Full-Service Travel Agents

More and more, full-service agencies are focusing on cruising due to its growing popularity. And while many full-service agencies may not have the best cruise discounts at their fingertips, they may know where to look and how to negotiate with a cruise line for a good rate. When calling full-service agencies, look for one that has a "cruise" desk with agents who sell only cruises. Avoid agencies that try to steer you toward a land vacation instead of the cruise you really want.

Spotting Swindlers

Although one is far more likely to encounter incompetent travel agents than scam artists, it's important to be on the lookout for a con. The best way to avoid being fleeced, if you don't have an established relationship with a travel agent, is to pay for your cruise with a credit card, from deposit to full payment. That way, if an agency goes out of business before your cruise departs, you can cancel payment on services not rendered. An agency may be a bad apple if it doesn't accept credit cards. Also be wary of any agency that wants an unusually high deposit (check the brochure). To avoid a disreputable agency, make sure the one you choose has been in business for at least five years. Check its reputation with the local Better Business Bureau or state consumer protection agency *before* you pay any deposits. If a cruise price seems too good to be true, it probably is. It could mean the agency is desperate to bring in money and may close its doors tomorrow. So be wary of agencies that claim they can beat any price.

Getting the Best Cruise for Your Dollar

By selecting the right agent, you have the greatest chance of getting the best deal. But having a basic knowledge of how and why cruises are discounted can only benefit you in the end. Since your vacation experience can vary greatly depending on the ship and its ports of call, it's best to pick your vessel and itinerary first, and then try to get the best price. Remember, it's only a deal if the cruise you book, no matter what the price, meets your expectations.

Like everything in retail, each cruise has a brochure list price. But like the sticker price on a new car, nobody actually pays this amount. These days, if you asked any 10 cruise passengers on any given ship what they paid, they would give you 10 different answers. Discounts from cruise lines and agencies can range from 5% on a single fare to 50% on the second fare in a cabin.

Approach deep discounts with skepticism. Fewer than a dozen cabins may be offered at the discounted price, they may be inside cabins, and the fare may not include air transportation or transfers between the airport and the ship. Finally, do the math. A promotion might sound catchy, but if you divide the price by the number of days you'll be cruising and include the cost of air and accommodations, you might find that the deal of the century is really a dud.

Deals and Discounts
SEASONAL DISCOUNTS
Cruise-brochure prices are typically divided into three categories based on the popularity of sailing dates and weather: high season, shoulder season, and low-season. Before you take advantage of a low-season rate, think about the pros and cons of off-season travel. It may be hotter (or colder) than you'd prefer—but it also may be less crowded.

EARLY-BIRD SPECIALS
More than ever, it's important to book early. This is especially true for the newest ships and for cabins with private verandas—both are selling out quickly. If you wait to book, you'll probably pay more even if you don't get shut out from the ship or cabin of your choice. That's because almost all cruise lines provide a discount for passengers who book and put down a deposit far in advance; an additional discount may be provided if payment is made in full at the time of booking. These discounts, given to passengers who book at least six months before departure, range from 10% to 50% off the brochure rate. (Brochures are usually issued a year or more in advance of sailing dates.)

As the sailing date approaches, the price of a cruise tends to go up. Not only that, but as the ship fills, the best cabins are no longer available and you'll be less likely to get the meal seating of your choice. So it certainly pays to book early.

LAST-MINUTE SAVINGS

In recent years, cruise lines have provided fewer and fewer last-minute deals. However, if a particular cruise is not selling well, a cruise line may pick certain large cruise-only travel agencies to unload unsold cabins. Keep in mind that your choice of cabin and meal seating is limited for such last-minute deals. On older ships—those built before the 1980s—special deals may be limited to smaller cabins in undesirable areas of the ship. Last-minute deals may be available only to people living in certain cities. Typically, these specials are unadvertised, but they may be listed in the agencies' newsletters and on their cruise telephone hot lines (*see* Agencies to Contact, *below*).

MIXED BAG

Besides the major discounts mentioned above, agencies and cruise lines might attract passengers with price promotions such as "Sail for 12 Days and Pay for Only 10," "Free Hotel Stay with Your Cruise," and "Two Sail for the Price of One." Read the fine print before you book. The offer may be a bargain—or just slick advertising. How can you tell? Compare the advertised price to the standard early-booking discount, and check if the promotion includes airfare. Also check on senior-citizen discounts and "cruise dollars" accrued on participating credit cards. Cruise lines that target families sometimes take on a third or fourth cabin passenger for free.

UPGRADES

There are two types of cabin upgrades: One is guaranteed; the other is not. The first kind of upgrade is a promotional offer by the cruise line. For example, you may be offered a two-category upgrade if you book by a certain date. In this case, the cabin assignment that you receive with your documents prior to sailing should reflect your better accommodations. The second kind of upgrade is dispensed on board at the discretion of the cruise line. Like airlines, cruise lines overbook at their cheapest price in order to attract as many passengers as possible. When the number of bookings at these low rates exceeds the number of cabins available, some people are given better accommodations.

How does the cruise line decide? Sometimes, those passengers who booked early get priority for upgrades. Other times, passengers who booked through top-selling travel agencies are at the top of the upgrade list—just two more reasons to book early and book with a cruise-only agency that does a lot of business with your line.

Payment

Once you have made a reservation for a cabin, you will be asked to put down a deposit. Handing money over to your travel agent constitutes a contract, so before you pay, review the cruise brochure to find out the provisions of the cruise contract. What is the payment schedule and cancellation policy? Will there be any additional charges before you can board your ship, such as transfers, port fees, or local taxes? If your air connection requires you to spend an evening in a hotel near the port before or after the cruise, is there an extra cost?

If possible, pay your deposit and balance with a credit card. This gives you some recourse if you need to cancel, and you can ask the credit-card company to intercede on your behalf in case of problems.

Deposit

Most cruises must be reserved with a refundable deposit of $200–$500 per person, depending upon how expensive the cruise is; the balance is due 45–75 days before you sail. If the cruise is less than 60 days away, however, you may have to pay the entire amount immediately.

Cancellation

Your entire deposit or payment may be refunded if you cancel your reservation between 45 and 75 days before departure; the grace period varies from line to line. If you cancel later than that, you will forfeit some or all of your deposit (*see* Insurance, *below*). An average cancellation charge is $100 one month before sailing, $100 plus 50% of the ticket price between 15 and 30 days prior to departure, and $100 plus 75% of the ticket price between 14 days and 24 hours ahead of time. If you simply fail to show up when the ship sails, you will lose the entire amount. Many travel agents also assess a small cancellation fee. Check their policy.

Insurance

Travel insurance is the best way to protect yourself against financial loss. The most useful plan is a comprehensive policy that includes coverage for trip cancellation-and-interruption, cruise line default, trip delay (including missed cruise connections), and medical expenses (with a waiver for pre-existing conditions).

Always buy travel insurance directly from the insurance company; if you buy it from a cruise line that goes out of business, your default coverage will be invalid.

TRAVEL INSURERS

In the U.S., **Access America** (6600 W. Broad St., Richmond, VA 23230, tel. 804/285–3300 or 800/284–8300). **Travel Guard International** (1145 Clark St., Stevens Point, WI 54481, tel. 715/345–0505 or 800/826–1300). In Canada, **Mutual of Omaha** (Travel Division, 500 University Ave., Toronto, Ontario M5G 1V8, tel. 416/598–4083; 800/268–8825 in Canada).

Agencies to Contact

The agencies listed below specialize in booking cruises, have been in business at least five years, and emphasize customer service as well as price.

CRUISE ONLY

Cruise Fairs of America (2029 Century Park E, Suite 950, Los Angeles, CA 90067, tel. 310/556–2925 or 800/456–4386, fax 310/556–2254), established in 1987, has a faxback service for information on the latest deals. The agency also publishes a free quarterly newsletter with tips on cruising. Cruise Fairs can make independent hotel and air arrangements for a complete cruise vacation.

Cruise Holidays of Kansas City (7000 N.W. Prairie View Rd., Kansas City, MO 64151, tel. 816/741–7417 or 800/869–6806, fax 816/741–7123), a franchisee of Cruise Holidays, a cruise-only agency with outlets throughout the United States, has been in business since 1988. The agency mails out a free newsletter to clients every other month with listings of cruise bargains—its prices are among the best.

Cruise Line, Inc. (150 N.W. 168th St., N. Miami Beach, FL 33169, tel. 305/653–6111 or 800/777–0707, fax 305/

653–6228), established in 1983, publishes *World of Cruising* magazine three times a year and a number of free brochures, including "Guide to First Time Cruising," "Guide to Family Cruises," "Guide to Exotic Cruising," and "Guide to Cruise Ship Weddings and Honeymoons." The agency has a 24-hour hot line with prerecorded cruise deals that are updated weekly.

Cruise Pro (2527 E. Thousand Oaks Blvd., Thousand Oaks, CA 91362, tel. 805/371–9884 or 800/222–7447; 800/258–7447 in CA; fax 805/371–9084), established in 1983, has special discounts listed in its one time per-month mailings to members of its Voyager's Club ($15 to join).

CruiseMasters (300 Corporate Pointe, Suite 100, Culver City, CA 90230, tel. 310/568–2040 or 800/242–9000, fax 310/568–2044), established in 1987, gives each passenger a personalized, bound guide to their ship's ports of call. The guides provide money-saving tips and advice on whether to opt for a prepackaged port excursion or strike out on your own.

Cruises, Inc. (5000 Campuswood Dr., E. Syracuse, NY 10357, tel. 315/463–9695 or 800/854–0500, fax 315/434–9175) opened its doors in 1981 and now has nearly 200 cruise consultants, including many CLIA Master Cruise Counsellors and Accredited Cruise Counsellors. Its agents are extensively trained and have extensive cruise experience. They sell a lot of cruises, which means the company gets very good prices from the cruise lines. Customer-service extras include complimentary accident insurance for up to $250,000 per cruise, a monthly bargain bulletin ($19 a yr), and a free twice-a-year cruise directory with cruise reviews, tips, and discounts.

Cruises of Distinction (2750 S. Woodward Ave., Bloomfield Hills, MI 48304, tel. 248/332–2020 or 800/634–3445, fax 248/333–9710), established in 1984, publishes a free 80-page cruise catalog four times a year. For no fee you can receive notification of unadvertised specials by mail or fax—just by filling out a questionnaire.

Don Ton Cruise Tours (3151 Airway Ave., E–1, Costa Mesa, CA 92626, tel. 714/545–3737 or 800/318–1818, fax 714/545–5275), established in 1972, features a variety of special-interest clubs, including a short-notice club, singles club, family cruise club, and adventure cruise club. Its "CruiseNet" magazine is filled with articles as well as price discounts six times a year.

Golden Bear Travel (16 Digital Dr., Novato, CA 94949, tel. 415/382–8900; 800/551–1000 outside CA; fax 415/382–9086) acts as general sales agent for a number of foreign cruise ships and specializes in longer, luxury cruises. Its Cruise Value club sends members free twice-a-month mailings with special prices on "distressed merchandise" cruises that are not selling well. The agency's Mariner Club (for past passengers) offers discounts on sailings and runs escorted cruises for people who would like to travel as part of a group.

Kelly Cruises (1315 W. 22nd St., Suite 105, Oak Brook, IL 60521, tel. 630/990–1111 or 800/837–7447, fax 630/990–1147), established in 1986, publishes a quarterly newsletter highlighting new ships and special rates. Passengers can put their name on a free mailing list for last-minute deals. Kelly is especially good if you're interested in the more expensive cruise lines.

National Discount Cruise Co. (1409 N. Cedar Crest Blvd., Allentown, PA 18104, tel. 610/439–4883 or 800/788–8108, fax 610/439–8086) is a five-year-old cruise division launched by GTA Travel, an American Express representative that has served travelers since 1967. The cruise division specializes in high-end cruises and includes shipboard credits, exclusive to American Express, on most of the sailings it books. A three-times-a-year newsletter highlights the agency's latest discounts.

Ship 'N' Shore Cruises (1160 S. McCall Rd., Englewood, FL 34223, tel. 941/475–5414 or 800/925–7447, fax 800/346–4119), an American Express representative founded in 1987, specializes in affordable cruise-tours around the world. In Alaska, the agency has its own fleet of motor coaches, and its land tours are custom-designed to complement the cruise itineraries of Alaska's major cruise lines.

Vacations at Sea (4919 Canal St., New Orleans, LA 70119, tel. 504/482–1572 or 800/749–4950, fax 504/486–8360), established in 1983, puts together its own pre- and post-cruise land packages and escorted land tours. The agency also publishes a free six-times-a-year newsletter with cruise reviews and discounts.

Ambassador Tours (717 Market St., San Francisco, CA 94103, tel. 415/357-9876 or 800/989–9000, fax 415/357-9667), established in 1955, does 80% of its business in cruises. Three times a year, the agency distributes a free 32-page catalog, which lists discounts on cruises and land packages, plus free monthly discount alerts.

Mann Travel and Cruises (6010 Fairview Rd., Suite 104, Charlotte, NC 28210, tel. 704/556–8311, fax 704/556–8303), established in 1975, does 65% of its business in cruises. The agency's cruise business has increased so much they recently added the word "cruises" to their name.

Prestige Travel (6175 Spring Mountain Rd., Las Vegas, NV 89102, tel. 702/248–1300, fax 702/253–6316), established in 1981, does 60% of it business in cruises. The agency holds an annual trade show for all its local clients, publishes a quarterly travel catalog, and sends frequent mailings to past customers.

Time to Travel (582 Market St., San Francisco, CA 94104, tel. 415/421–3333 or 800/524–3300, fax 415/421–4857), established in 1935, does 90% of its business in cruises. It mails a free listing of cruise discounts to its clients three to five times a month. Time to Travel specializes in pre- and post-cruise land arrangements and claims its staff of 19 has been nearly everywhere in the world.

White Travel Service (127 Park Rd., West Hartford, CT 06119, tel. 860/233–2648 or 800/547–4790; 860/236–6176 prerecorded cruise hot line with discount listings; fax 860/236–6177), founded in 1972, does most of its business in cruises and publishes a free 40-page brochure listing the latest cruise discounts.

BEFORE YOU GO

Tickets, Vouchers, and Other Travel Documents

After you make the final payment to your travel agent, the cruise line will issue your cruise tickets and vouchers for airport–ship transfers. Depending on the airline, and whether you have purchased an air-sea package, you may receive your plane tickets or charter-flight vouchers at the same time; you may also receive vouchers for any shore excursions, although most cruise lines issue these aboard ship. Should your travel documents not arrive when promised, contact your travel agent or call the cruise line directly. If you book late, tickets may be delivered directly to the ship.

What to Pack

Certain packing rules apply to all cruises: Always take along a sweater in case of cool evening ocean breezes or overactive air-conditioning. A rain slicker usually comes in handy, too, and make sure you take at least one pair of comfortable walking shoes for exploring port towns. Men should pack a dark suit, a tuxedo, or a white dinner jacket. Women should pack one long gown or cocktail dress for every two or three formal evenings on board. Most ships have semi-formal evenings, when men should wear a jacket and tie.

Generally speaking, plan on one outfit for every two days of cruising, especially if your wardrobe contains many interchangeable pieces. Ships often have convenient laundry facilities as well. And don't overload your luggage with extra toiletries and sundry items; they are easily available in port and in the ship's gift shop (though usually at a premium price). Soaps, and sometimes shampoos and body lotion, are often placed in your cabin compliments of the cruise line.

Take an extra pair of eyeglasses or contact lenses in your carry-on luggage. If you have a health problem that requires a prescription drug, pack enough to last the duration of the trip or have your doctor write a prescription using the drug's generic name, because brand names vary from country to country. Always carry prescription drugs in their original packaging to avoid problems with customs officials. Don't pack them in luggage that you plan to check in case your bags go astray. Pack a list of the offices that supply refunds for lost or stolen traveler's checks.

ARRIVING AND DEPARTING

If you have purchased an air-sea package, you will be met by a cruise-company representative when your plane lands at the port city and then shuttled directly to the ship in buses or minivans. Some cruise lines arrange to transport your luggage between airport and ship—you don't have to hassle with baggage claim at the start of your cruise or with baggage check-in at the end. If you decide not to buy the air-sea package but still plan to fly, ask your travel agent if you can use the ship's transfer bus anyway; if you do, you may be required to purchase a round-trip transfer voucher ($5–$20). Otherwise, you will have to take a taxi to the ship.

If you live close to the port of embarkation, bus transportation may be available. If you are part of a group that has booked a cruise together, this transportation may be part of your package. Another option for those who live close to their point of departure is to drive to the ship. The major U.S. cruise ports all have parking facilities.

Embarkation

Check-In

On arrival at the dock, you must check in before boarding your ship. (A handful of smaller cruise ships handle check-in at the airport.) An officer will collect or stamp your ticket, inspect or even retain your passport or other official identification, ask you to fill out a tourist card, check that you have the correct visas, and collect any unpaid port or departure tax. Seating assignments for the dining room are often handed out at this time, too. You may also register your credit card to open a shipboard account, although that may be done later at the purser's office.

After this you may be required to go through a security check and to pass your hand baggage through an X-ray inspection. These are the same machines in use at airports, so ask to have your photographic film inspected visually.

Although it takes only five or 10 minutes per family to check in, lines are often long, so aim for off-peak hours. The worst time tends to be immediately after the ship begins boarding; the later it is, the less crowded. For example, if boarding begins at 2 PM and continues until 4:30, try to arrive after 3:30.

Boarding the Ship

Before you walk up the gangway, the ship's photographer will probably take your picture; there's no charge unless you buy the picture (usually $6). On board, stewards may serve welcome drinks in souvenir glasses—for which you're usually charged between $3 and $5 cash.

You will either be escorted to your cabin by a steward or, on a smaller ship, given your key by a ship's officer and directed to your cabin. Some elevators are unavailable to passengers during boarding, since they are used to transport luggage. You may arrive to find your luggage outside your stateroom or just inside the door; if it doesn't arrive within a half hour before sailing, contact the purser. If you are among the unlucky few whose luggage doesn't make it to the ship in time, the purser will trace it and arrange to have it flown to the next port.

Visitors' Passes

Some cruise ships permit passengers to invite guests on board prior to sailing, although most cruise lines prohibit all but paying passengers for reasons of security and insurance liability. Cruise companies that allow visitors usually require that you obtain passes several weeks in advance; call the lines for policies and procedures.

Most ships do not allow visitors while the ship is docked in a port of call. If you meet a friend on shore, you won't be able to invite him or her back to your stateroom.

Disembarkation

The last night of your cruise is full of business. On most ships you must place everything except your hand luggage outside your cabin door, ready to be picked up by midnight. Color-coded tags, distributed to your cabin in a debarkation packet, should be placed on your luggage before the crew collects it. Your designated color will later determine when you leave the ship and help you retrieve your luggage on the pier.

Your shipboard bill is left in your room during the last day; to pay the bill (if you haven't already put it on your credit card) or to settle any questions, you must stand in line at the purser's office. Tips to the cabin steward and dining staff are distributed on the last night.

The next morning, in-room breakfast service is usually not available because stewards are too busy. Most passengers clear out of their cabins as soon as possible, gather their hand luggage, and stake out a chair in one of the public lounges to await the ship's clearance through customs. Be patient—it takes a long time to unload and sort thousands of pieces of luggage. Passengers are disembarked by groups according to the color-coded tags placed on luggage the night before; those with the earliest flights get off first. If you have a tight connection, notify the purser before the last day, and he or she may be able to arrange faster preclearing and debarkation for you.

2 Ports of Call

GOING ASHORE

Traveling by cruise ship presents an opportunity to visit many different places in a short time. The flip side is that your stay will be limited in each port of call. For that reason, cruise lines invented shore excursions, which maximize passengers' time by organizing their touring for them. There are a number of advantages to shore excursions: In some destinations, transportation may be unreliable, and a ship-packaged tour is the best way to see distant sights. Also, you don't have to worry about being stranded or missing the ship. The disadvantage is that you will pay more for the convenience of having the ship do the legwork for you. Of course, you can always book a tour independently, hire a taxi, or use foot power to explore on your own.

Disembarking

When your ship arrives in a port, it either ties up alongside a dock or anchors out in a harbor. If the ship is docked, passengers just walk down the gangway to go ashore. Docking makes it easy to go back and forth between the shore and the ship.

Tendering

If your ship anchors in the harbor, however, you will have to take a small boat—called a launch or tender—to get ashore. Tendering is a nuisance. When your ship first arrives in port, everyone wants to go ashore. Often, in order to avoid a stampede at the tenders, you must gather in a public room, get a boarding pass, and wait until your number is called. This continues until everybody has disembarked. Even then, it may take 15–20 minutes to get ashore if your ship is anchored far offshore. Because tenders can be difficult to board, passengers with mobility problems may not be able to visit certain ports. The larger the ship, the more likely it will use tenders. It is usually possible to learn before booking a cruise whether the ship will dock or anchor at its ports of call. (For more information about where and whether ships dock, tender, or both, *see* Coming Ashore for each port, *below*.)

Before anyone is allowed to walk down the gangway or board a tender, the ship must first be cleared for landing. Immigration and customs officials board the vessel to examine passports and sort through red tape. It may be more than an hour before you're actually allowed ashore. You will be issued a boarding pass, which you must have with you to get back on board.

Returning to the Ship

Cruise lines are strict about sailing times, which are posted at the gangway and elsewhere as well as announced in the daily schedule of activities. Be certain to be back on board at least a half hour before the announced sailing time or you may be stranded. If you are on a shore excursion that was sold by the cruise line, however, the captain will wait for your group before casting off. That is one reason many passengers prefer ship-packaged tours.

If you are not on one of the ship's tours and the ship does sail without you, immediately contact the cruise line's port representative, whose name and phone number are often listed on the daily schedule of activities. You may be able to hitch a ride on a pilot boat, though that is unlikely. Passengers who miss the boat must pay their own way to the next port of call.

ALASKA

Alaska, it would seem, was made for cruising. The traditional route to the state is by sea, through a 1,000-mi-long protected waterway known as the Inside Passage. From Vancouver in the south to Skagway in the north, the Inside Passage winds around islands large and small, past glacier-carved fjords, and along hemlock-blanketed mountains. This great land is home to breaching whales, nesting eagles, spawning salmon, and calving glaciers. Most towns here can be reached only by air or sea; there are no roads. Juneau, in fact, is the only water-locked state capital in the United States. Beyond the Inside Passage, the Gulf of Alaska leads to Prince William Sound—famous for its marine life and more fjords and glaciers—and Anchorage, Alaska's largest city.

Alaska Cruising Region

Anchorage
Whittier
KENAI MTS.
Seward
Valdez
GLENN HWY.
Klondike R.
Dawson
YUKON TERRITORY
College Fjord
Prince William Sound
Mt. St. Elias
ALASKA RANGE
ALASKA HWY.
Icy Bay
Gulf of Alaska
Whitehorse
Carcross
PACIFIC OCEAN
Haines
Skagway
Glacier Bay National Park and Preserve
Juneau
BRITISH COLUMBIA
Sitka
Baranof Island
Inside Passage
Petersburg
Wrangell
Misty Fjords National Monument
Revillagigedo Island
Ketchikan
Prince Rupert
Peace River
Queen Charlotte Islands
Fraser R.

N

| 0 | | 250 | miles |
| 0 | | 375 | km |

Vancouver Island
Vancouver
Victoria

KEY
Ports of Call
Rail Lines

Natural beauty is just one reason why so many cruise passengers now set sail for Alaska. The peak season falls during summer school vacation, so kids are now a common sight aboard ship. Cruise lines have responded with programs designed specifically for children, and some discount shore excursions for kids under 12.

For adults, too, the cruise lines now offer more than ever before. Alaska is one of cruising's hottest destinations, so the lines are putting their newest, biggest ships up here. These gleaming vessels have the best facilities at sea. Fully equipped, top-deck health spas give panoramic views of the passing scenery. Some ships feature onboard broadcasts of CNN and ESPN or sports bars showing live televised events. New itineraries give passengers more choices than ever before, too—from Bering Strait cruises, which include a crossing to the Russian Far East, to 10-, 11-, and 14-day loop cruises of the Inside Passage, round-trip from Vancouver. Shorter cruises focus on Glacier Bay or equally scenic Prince William Sound.

You will still find all the time-honored diversions of a vacation at sea aboard Alaska-bound ships. Daily programs schedule bingo and bridge tournaments, deck games, and various contests, demonstrations, and lectures. You'll also find trendier pursuits: Some lines have stress-management seminars and talks on financial planning.

Food remains a major reason to visit Alaska aboard a cruise ship. On the big ocean liners, you can eat practically all day and night. Along with prime rib now comes a selection of healthful choices for nutrition-conscious eaters. Some ships offer a "spa menu," which ties your dining-room meals together with your exercise program in the health club.

Nearly every day, your ship will make a port call. With the exception of Anchorage, Alaskan port cities are small and easily explored by foot. For those who prefer to be shown the sights, ship-organized shore excursions are available. These range from typical city bus tours to Alaska's most exciting excursion adventure: helicopter flightseeing with a landing on a glacier. Other choices include charter fishing, river rafting, and visits to Native American communities. To satisfy the interest of their ever-younger and more active passengers, Alaska's cruise lines constantly refine their shore-excursion programs, adding new educational and adventure-oriented choices. The programs change annually, as the lines search for just the right mix of leisure and learning (*see* Shore Excursions, *below*).

Itineraries

About a dozen major cruise lines deploy ships in Alaska. Sailings come chiefly in two varieties: round-trip Inside Passage loops or one-way Inside Passage–Gulf of Alaska cruises. Both itineraries are typically seven days. However, if you want to combine a land tour with your Inside Passage loop, you can only spend three or four days aboard ship. On the other hand, Inside Passage–Gulf of Alaska cruises allow you to spend a full week aboard ship and still take a pre- or post-cruise land tour. A few lines schedule longer one-way or round-trip sailings from Vancouver or San Francisco.

Whether you sail through the Inside Passage or along it will depend upon the size of your vessel. Smaller ships can navigate narrow channels, straits, and fjords. Larger vessels must sail farther from land, so don't expect to see much wildlife from the deck of a megaship.

Cruise Tours

Most cruise lines give you the option of an independent, hosted, or fully escorted land tour before or after your cruise. Independent tours allow maximum flexibility. You have a preplanned itinerary with confirmed hotel reservations and transportation arrangements, but you're free to follow your interests and whims in each town. A hosted tour is similar, but tour company representatives are available along the route to help out should you need assistance.

On fully escorted tours, you travel with a group, led by a tour director. Activities are preplanned (and typically prepaid) so you have a good idea of how much your trip will cost (not counting incidentals) before you depart.

Modes of tour transportation range from plane to bus, rail to ferry. Most cruise tour itineraries include a ride aboard the Alaska Railroad in a private, glass-domed railcar. Running between Anchorage, Denali National Park, and Fairbanks, Holland America Westours' *McKinley Explorer* and Princess Tours' *Midnight Sun Express Ultra Dome* offer unobstructed views of the passing land and wildlife.

In addition to full-length cruise-tours, cruise lines usually sell pre- or post-cruise packages lasting one to three days. Hotel accommodations and some sightseeing in port cities are generally included.

When to Go

The Alaska cruise season runs from spring through fall, but midsummer departures are the most popular. Cruise lines schedule first sailings in mid-May and final sailings in late September. May and June are the driest summer months, but you should still come prepared for rain, especially in Southeast Alaska. At least two cruise lines price sailings by six or seven "seasons," with spring and fall departures the least expensive and midsummer sailings the most costly. Virtually every line offers early-booking discounts to passengers for advance deposits.

There are plenty of advantages besides discounted fares to cruising in the low seasons. Availability of ships and particular cabins is greater in the low and shoulder seasons and the ports are almost completely empty of tourists. In spring, wildflowers are abundant. You're apt to see more wildlife along the shore, because the animals have not yet gone up to higher elevations. Alaska's early fall brings the splendor of autumn hues and the first snow falls in the mountains. The animals have returned to low ground, and shorter days bring the possibility of seeing the northern lights. Mosquitoes are also not as thick in the fall, a decided plus.

Temperatures along the Southeast Alaska cruise routes are in the 50s and 60s in May, June, and September. In July and August averages are generally in the 60s and low 70s. Southcentral Alaska has warmer temperatures, with many midsummer days in the mid-70s. For passengers opting to take a cruise-tour (a combination of cruising and land touring that is popular in Alaska), the Interior section of the state—where you'll find Mt. McKinley—often reaches into the 80s, with occasional days topping 90 degrees.

Shore Excursions

Shore excursions in Alaska give cruise passengers a chance to get closer to the state's natural beauty. For this reason, active or adventure-oriented tours are usually the best choices. Not all shore excursions are offered by every ship. However, you can book any excursion directly; try calling one of the ground operators listed below (*see* Independent Touring, *below*).

AERIAL TOURS

Anyone unwilling to hike or boat in the backcountry should take at least one small-plane or helicopter tour to see the state in its full glory. The aircraft fly over glaciers and waterways, with floatplanes landing on wilderness lakes. Some helicopter tours actually land on a glacier and let passengers out to do some brief exploring.

FISHING

The prospect of bringing a trophy salmon or halibut to net is one reason many people choose an Alaskan cruise. Every ship offers optional fishing excursions on charter boats.

HIKING

Trekking through woods and mountains and along the beaches is a popular pastime in Southeast Alaska. Some trails are abandoned mining roads; others are natural routes or game trails that meander over ridges, through forests, and alongside streams and glaciers. Many ships offer hiking excursions, but every port is within easy access of at least some hiking. Trails go through real wilderness, so check with local public information centers for current conditions, and leave your intended itinerary with someone on the ship. Look under the hiking section for each port to find trails and paths convenient to cruise passengers.

SALMON BAKE

Alaska is famous for outdoor salmon barbecues, called salmon bakes. Fresh fish is grilled on an open fire and served with plenty of fixings. Quality varies, so ask locals for advice on which bake to attend. Juneau has one of the best: the Gold Creek Salmon Bake, which is sold as a shore excursion by virtually every cruise line.

WHALE-WATCHING

Whales are plentiful in these waters, and several small-boat excursions offer excellent opportunities to see them up close. Humpback whales are often seen in the waters near Glacier Bay National Park, but you may also see the smaller minke whales and killer whales (orcas). Beluga whales are frequently observed in Cook Inlet near Anchorage—but few ships sail that far north.

Independent Touring

As noted below, not all shore excursions recommended in this chapter are offered by all cruise lines. Some passengers may also choose to make arrangements on their own to avoid the cruise-line markup. To book shore excursions directly, contact these companies:

IN ANCHORAGE

For flightseeing or fly-in fishing trips contact **Rust's Flying Service** (tel. 907/243–1595 or 800/544–2299), **Regal Air** (tel. 907/243–8535), or **Ketchum Air Service** (tel. 907/243–5525 or 800/433–9114). For a glacier and wildlife viewing tour in Prince William Sound, contact **Phillips Cruises and Tours** (tel. 907/276–8023 or 800/544–0529), **Renown Charters and Tours** (tel. 907/272–1961 or 800/655–3806), or **Major Marine Tours** (tel. 907/274–7300 or 800/764–7300). For a trip north to Talkeetna or south to Seward, contact the **Alaska Railroad** (tel. 907/265–2494 or 800/544–0552). For historic walking tours of downtown, contact **Anchorage Historic Properties** (tel. 907/274–3600); **Anchorage City Trolley Tours** (tel. 907/257–5603) offers the motorized version.

IN HAINES

Try **Mountain Flying Service** (tel. 907/766–3007) or **Haines Airways** (tel. 907/766–2646) for flightseeing tours. For local bike tours contact **Sockeye Cycle** (tel. 907/766–2869), and for float trips down the Chilkat River contact **Chilkat Guides** (tel. 907/ 766-2491).

IN HOMER

Contact **Homer Air** (tel. 907/235–8591 or 800/235–8591), **Southcentral Air** (tel. 907/235–6172 or 800/478–6172), or **Bald Mountain Air Service** (tel. 907/235–7969 or 800/478–7969) for flightseeing tours. For local sightseeing contact **Homer Tours** (tel. 907/235–6200). For wildlife watching contact **Rainbow Tours** (tel. 907/235–7272) or **Alaska Maritime Tours** (tel. 907/235-2490 or 800/478-2490). The **Homer Chamber of Commerce** (tel. 907/235–7740) has a complete list of fishing charter boats.

IN JUNEAU

For flightseeing contact two longtime favorites: **Ward Air** (tel. 907/789–9150) or **Alaska Coastal Airlines** (tel. 907/789–7818). Other air taxi operators include **Wings of Alaska** (tel. 907/789–0790) and **L.A.B. Flying Service** (tel. 907/789–9160 or 800/426–0543). Both **Era Helicopters** (tel. 907/586–2030 or 800/843–1947) and **Temsco Helicopters** (tel. 907/789–9501) offer tours that include a glacier landing. For local sightseeing contact **Alaska Native Tours** (907/463–3231). For Mendenhall River float trips call **Alaska Discovery** (tel. 907/780–6226 or 800/586–1911).

IN KETCHIKAN

For flightseeing contact **Taquan Air** (tel. 907/225–9668 or 800/770–8800), **Island Wings Air Service** (tel. 907/225–2444 or 888/854–2444), or **ProMech Air** (tel. 907/225–3845). For on-the-water adventures contact **Southeast Exposure** (tel. 907/225–8829), **Outdoor Alaska** (tel. 907/225–6044), or **Southeast Sea Kayaks** (tel. 907/225–1258). Native cultural tours are offered by **Saxman Native Village** (tel. 907/225–5163) and the **Ketchikan Indian Corporation** (tel. 907/225–5158 or 800/252–5158).

IN PETERSBURG

Contact **Pacific Wing** (tel. 907/772–9258), **Nash West** Aviation (tel. 907/772–3344), or **Kupreanof Flying Service** (tel. 907/772–3396) for flightseeing. For a kayak trip up Petersburg creek, contact **Tongass Kayak Adventures** (tel. 907/772–4600). The **Petersburg Visitors Center** (tel. 907/772–4636) has a complete list of local fishing boats and operators for other activities.

IN SEWARD

For flightseeing contact **Scenic Mountain Air** (tel. 907/224–7277). **Kayak and Custom Adventures Worldwide** (tel. 907/276–8282 or 800/288–3134) offers kayak rentals and sea-kayak day trips. For fishing charters contact **Fish House** (tel. 907/224–3674 or 800/257–7760).

IN SITKA

For flightseeing contact **Mountain Aviation** (tel. 907/966–2288). For sightseeing and historical walking tours, contact **Tribal Tours** (907/747–7290 or 888/270–8687). For soft adventure, sea kayaking trips contact **Baidarka Boats** (tel. 907/747–8996).

Contact **Skagway Air** (tel. 907/983–2218), **Wings of Alaska** (tel. 907/983–2442), **L.A.B. Flying Service** (tel. 907/789–9160 or 800/426–0543), or **Temsco Helicopters** (tel. 907/789–9501) for flightseeing. For local sightseeing contact **Skagway Street Car Company** (tel. 907/983–2908).

For flightseeing contact **BMH Aviation** (tel. 907/255–8359) or **Era Helicopters** (tel. 907/835–2595 or 800/843–1947). For local sightseeing contact **Valdez Tours** (tel. 907/835–2686) or **Sentimental Journeys** (tel. 907/835–4988). For soft-adventure tours contact **Anadyr Seakayaking Adventures** (tel. 907/835–2814), **Northern Magic Charters** (tel. 800/835–4433), or **Stan Stephens Charters** (tel. 907/835–4731 or 800/992–1297).

Saloons

Socializing at a bar or saloon is an old Alaska custom, and the towns and cities of the Southeast Panhandle are no exception. Listed under the individual ports of call are some of the favorite gathering places in these parts.

Sea Kayaking

More adventurous travelers will enjoy paddling sea kayaks in the protected waters of Southeast and Southcentral Alaska. Ketchikan, Homer, Juneau, Seward, Sitka, and Valdez all have companies that rent sea kayaks, with lessons and short kayak tours available. Gear is usually provided.

Shopping

Alaskan Native American handicrafts range from Tlingit totem poles—a few inches high to several feet tall—to Athabascan beaded slippers and fur garments. Many other traditional pieces of art are found in gift shops up and down the coast: Inupiat spirit masks and intricately carved ivory, Yupik dolls and dance fans, Tlingit button blankets and silver jewelry, and Aleut grass baskets and carved wooden items. To ensure authenticity, buy items tagged with the state-approved AUTHENTIC NATIVE HANDCRAFT FROM ALASKA "Silverhand" label. Better prices are found in the more remote villages where you buy directly from the artisan, in museum shops, or in craft fairs such as Anchorage's downtown Saturday Market.

Salmon, halibut, crab, and other seafood are very popular with both locals and visitors. Most towns have a local company that packs and ships seafood.

Dining

Not surprisingly, seafood dominates most menus. In summer, salmon, halibut, crab, cod, and prawns are usually fresh. Restaurants are uniformly informal; jeans and windbreakers are the norm.

CATEGORY	COST*
$$$	over $40
$$	$20–$40
$	under $20

per person for a three-course meal, excluding drinks, service, and sales tax

Anchorage

A local newspaper columnist once dubbed Anchorage "a city too obviously on the make to ever be accepted in polite society." And for all its cosmopolitan trappings, this city of 240,000 people does maintain something of an opportunistic, pioneer spirit. Its inhabitants hustle for their living in the retail, transportation, communications, medical, oil, and education fields.

Superficially, Anchorage looks like any other sprawling western American city, with WalMarts and shopping malls, but sled-dog races are as popular here as surfing is in California, and moose occasionally roam along city bike trails. This is basically a modern, relatively unattractive city, but the Chugach Mountains form a striking backdrop, and spectacular Alaskan wilderness is found just outside the back door. Few people come to Alaska to see Anchorage, but almost everybody passes through sometime during their trip, and the city does have almost anything you may want, from Starbucks espresso to Native handicrafts.

Anchorage took shape with the construction of the federally built Alaska Railroad (completed in 1923), and traces of the city's railroad heritage remain. With the tracks laid, the town's pioneer forefathers actively sought expansion by hook and—not infrequently—by crook. City fathers, many of whom are still alive, delight in telling how they tricked a visiting U.S. congressman into dedicating the site for a federal hospital that had not yet been approved.

Boom and bust periods followed major events: an influx of military bases during World War II; a massive buildup of Arctic missile-warning stations during the Cold War; and more recently, the discovery of oil at Prudhoe Bay and the construction of the trans-Alaska pipeline.

Anchorage today is the only true metropolis in Alaska. There's a performing-arts center, a diversity of museums, and a variety of ethnic eateries for cruise passengers to sample.

Shore Excursions

Other than a typical city bus tour, few shore excursions are scheduled in Anchorage. Most cruise passengers are only passing through the city as they transfer between the airport and the ship or a land tour and their cruise. For passengers who arrive early or stay later, independently or on a pre- or post-cruise package, there is much to see and do (*see* Exploring Anchorage, *below*).

The following is a good choice in Anchorage. It may not be offered by all cruise lines. Times and prices are approximate.

Anchorage Highlights. This motor-coach tour visits the Museum of History and Art, then moves on to see the bears, moose, wolves, bald eagles, and other Alaskan wildlife at the city zoo. Before returning to the ship, the tour climbs the Chugach Mountains for panoramic views of Anchorage and then passes by the downtown historic area. *4 hrs. Cost: $29.*

Coming Ashore

Cruise ships visiting Anchorage most often dock at the port city of Seward, 125 mi to the south on the Kenai Peninsula; from here passengers must travel by bus or train to Anchorage. Ships that do sail directly to the city dock just beyond downtown. A tourist information booth is right on the pier. The major attractions are a 15- or 20-minute walk away; turn right when you disembark and head south on Ocean Dock Road. The main tourist district of downtown Anchorage is very easy to navigate on foot. If you want to see some of the outlying attractions, like Lake Hood (*see* Exploring, *below*), you'll need to hire a taxi. Taxis are expensive: Rates start at $2 for pickup and $1.50 for each mile (1½ km). Most people in Anchorage telephone for a cab, although it is not uncommon to hail one. Contact **Alaska Cab** (tel. 907/563–5353), **Anchorage Taxicab** (tel. 907/278–8000), **Checker Cab** (tel. 907/276–1234), or **Yellow Cab** (tel. 907/272–2422).

If you have the time and want to explore further afield, such as Girdwood and points south on the Kenai Peninsula, Anchorage is a great place to rent a car.

Exploring Anchorage
Numbers in the margin correspond to points of interest on the Downtown Anchorage map.

❶ A marker in front of the **Log Cabin Visitor Information Center** shows the mileage to various world cities. Fourth Avenue sustained heavy damage in the 1964 earthquake. The businesses on this block withstood the destruction, but those a block east fell into the ground as the earth under them slid toward Ship Creek. Most of these buildings have since been rebuilt. *Corner of 4th Ave. and F St., tel. 907/274–3531. Open summer, daily 7:30–7; spring and fall, daily 8–6.*

❷ Anchorage's real centerpiece is the distinctively modern **Performing Arts Center** at 5th Ave. and G Street. A diversity of musical, theatrical, and dance groups perform here throughout the year. Out front is flower-packed **Town Square,** a delightful place to relax on a sunny day.

❸ The Art Deco **Fourth Avenue Theater** (4th Ave. between F and G streets) has been restored and put to new use as a gift shop, café, and gallery. Note the lighted stars in the ceiling that form the Big Dipper against a field of blue—it's the Alaska state flag.

❹ Displays about Alaska's national parks, forests, and wildlife refuges can be seen at the **Alaska Public Lands Information Center.** The center also shows films highlighting different regions of the state and sells natural history books.

36

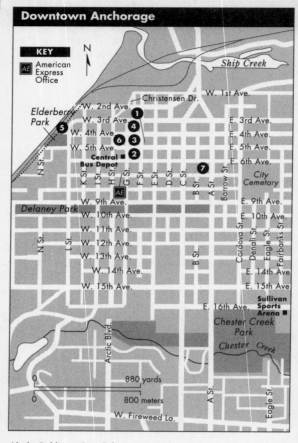

Downtown Anchorage

KEY

AE American Express Office

Ship Creek

Elderberry Park

Christensen Dr.

W. 1st Ave.
W. 2nd Ave.
W. 3rd Ave. — E. 3rd Ave.
W. 4th Ave. — E. 4th Ave.
W. 5th Ave. — E. 5th Ave.
E. 6th Ave.

Central Bus Depot

City Cemetery

W. 9th Ave. — E. 9th Ave.

Delaney Park

W. 10th Ave. — E. 10th Ave.
W. 11th Ave.
W. 12th Ave.
W. 13th Ave.
W. 14th Ave. — E. 14th Ave
W. 15th Ave. — E. 15th Ave

E. 16th Ave. — **Sullivan Sports Arena**

Chester Creek Park

Chester Creek

0   880 yards
0   800 meters

W. Fireweed La.

Alaska Public Lands Information Center, **4**

Anchorage Museum of History and Art, **7**

Fourth Avenue Theater, **3**

Imaginarium, **6**

Log Cabin Visitor Information Center, **1**

Oscar Anderson House, **5**

Performing Arts Center, **2**

4th Ave. and F St., tel. 907/271–2737. Open daily 9–5:30 in summer.

Resolution Park, a cantilevered viewing platform dominated by a monument to Captain Cook, looks out toward Cook Inlet and the mountains beyond. Mt. Susitna (known as the Sleeping Lady) is the prominent low mountain to the northwest. To her north, Mt. McKinley is often visible 125 mi away. (Most Alaskans prefer the traditional name for this peak, Denali.)

The paved **Tony Knowles Coastal Trail** runs along Cook Inlet for about 10 mi (16 km), and is accessible from the west end of 2nd Avenue. This is a wonderful place to take in the view, or to join the throngs of folks walking, running, biking, or rollerblading.

❺ The **Oscar Anderson House** is next to the trail at the north end of Elderberry Park. It was Anchorage's first permanent frame house, built in 1915. Tours are free. The park is also a good place to watch for porpoise-sized beluga whales in Cook Inlet. *Near 5th Ave. between L and N Sts., tel. 907/ 274–2336. Open Tues.–Sat. noon–4.*

❻ A fun stop for kids and adults alike is the **Imaginarium,** an interactive science museum with a great gift shop. *725 W. 5th Ave., tel. 907/276–3179. Admission: $5. Open Mon.– Sat. 10–6, Sun. noon–5.*

❼ The **Anchorage Museum of History and Art** occupies the whole block at 6th Avenue and A Street, with an entrance on 7th Avenue. It houses a fine collection of historical and contemporary Alaskan art, displays on Alaskan history, and a special section for children. One gallery is devoted to views of Alaska, as seen by early explorers, painters, and contemporary artists. *121 W. 7th Ave., tel. 907/343–4326. Admission: $5. Open daily 9–6.*

The new **Alaska Native Heritage Center** is scheduled to open in 1999 on the northeast side of Anchorage. On a 26-acre site facing the Chugach Mountains, this $15-million dollar facility includes a spacious Welcome House, where you are introduced to the Native peoples of Alaska through displays, artifacts, photographs, demonstrations, performances, and films. You can also circle a small lake and explore five

re-created village sites to learn more about Alaska's diverse
Native cultures. There's a café and Native arts gift shop as
well. *Glenn Hwy. and Muldoon Rd., tel. 907/263–5170.*

If you have the time, take a taxi to the **Lake Hood floatplane base,** where colorful aircraft come and go almost constantly in the summer months. The best vantage point is
from the patio of the lounge at the Regal Alaskan Hotel.
4800 Spenard Rd., tel. 907/243–2300.

Shopping

The **Alaska Native Arts and Crafts Association** sells items
from all Alaskan Native American groups and carries the
work of the best-known carvers, silversmiths, and bead
workers, as well as the work of unknown artists. *333 W.
4th Ave., tel. 907/274–2932. Open weekdays 10–7, Sat.
10–6, Sun. noon–5.*

The best buys on Native Alaskan artists' work are found
at the gift shop inside the **Alaska Native Medical Center.**
*Tudor Centre Dr. off East Tudor Rd., tel. 907/729–1122.
Open weekdays 10–2, 1st Sat. of month 10–2.*

Artwork created by Alaskan artists, both Native and non-
Native, can be found at **Artique Ltd.** (314 G St., tel. 907/
277–1663). The work of better-known Alaskan artists can
be seen at the **Decker/Morris Gallery** (corner of 7th Ave.
and G St. in the Performing Arts Center, tel. 907/272–1489).
For "wearable art" and one-of-a-kind designs in polar
fleece apparel, stop in at designer **Tracy Anna Bader's** bou-
tique (416 G St., tel. 907/272–6668). Another option for
warm wear is the **Oomingmak Musk Ox Producers Co-op**
(corner of 6th Ave. and H St., tel. 907/272–9225). Native
Alaskan villagers hand knit scarves and hats from the soft-
as-cashmere underwool of the musk ox into traditional designs. Another place for distinctive garments and parkas is
Laura Wright Alaskan Parkas (343 W. 5th Ave., tel. 907/
274–4215). The parkas are available off-the-rack or by custom order. Not far from here is **Cook Inlet Book Company**
(415 W. 5th Ave., tel. 907/258–4544), with a huge selection of Alaskan titles.

Wolf aficionados will enjoy a stop at **Wolf Song** (corner of
6th Ave. and C St., tel. 907/274–9653), a nonprofit gift shop
with wildlife art and educational material. The **Alaska**

General Store (715 W. 4th Ave., tel. 907/272–1672) gift shop is a browsers' delight, with an old fashioned ambience and a diverse collection of items, both old and new.

Anchorage's best places to buy fresh, frozen, or smoked seafood are not far from the center of town: **10th and M Seafoods** (1020 M St., tel. 907/272–6013), and **New Sagaya's City Market** (900 W. 13th Ave., tel. 907/274–6173). Both places will also ship seafood for you.

Entertainment
Take a goofy, off-kilter romp across Alaska at the "Whale Fat Follies" Tuesday through Saturday evenings in the **Fly By Night Club** (3300 Spenard Rd., tel. 907/279–7726). Mr. Whitekeys is the master of ceremonies for this musical extravaganza of bad taste and Spam jokes.

Jogging/Walking
The Tony Knowles Coastal Trail (*see* Exploring Anchorage, *above*) and other trails in Anchorage are used by cyclists, runners, and walkers. The trail from Westchester Lagoon at the end of 15th Avenue runs 2 mi (3 km) to Earthquake Park and, beyond that, 8 mi (13 km) out to Kincaid Park. For bike rentals, contact **Adventure Cafe** (K St. between 4th and 5th Aves., tel. 907/276–8282 or 800/288–3134) or **Downtown Bicycle Rental** (corner of 5th Ave. and C St., tel. 907/279–5293).

Dining
$$–$$$ **Club Paris.** It's dark and smoky up front in the bar, where for decades old-time Anchorage folks have met to drink and chat. Halibut and fried prawns are available, but the star attractions are the big, tender, flavorful steaks. If you have to wait for a table, have a drink at the bar and order the hors d'oeuvres tray—a sampler of steak, cheese, and prawns that could be a meal for two people. *417 W. 5th Ave., tel. 907/277–6332. AE, D, DC, MC, V.*

$$–$$$ **Marx Bros. Cafe.** Fusion cuisine served by chef Jack Amon shows that frontier cooking is much more than a kettle in the kitchen. Among the multicultural specialties of the house is baked halibut with a macadamia crust served with coconut curry and mango chutney. Reservations are essential—you might even want to call before you reach Anchorage. *627 W. 3rd Ave., tel. 907/278–2133. AE, DC, MC, V. No lunch.*

$$-$$$ **Sacks Cafe.** The downtown business crowd favors this bright little café. Delightfully creative soups, sandwiches, and salads fill the lunch menu, and for dinner, the kitchen produces such entrées as lamb braised in a spicy red curry sauce, and baked penne pasta with sun-dried tomatoes, spinach, roasted peppers, and three cheeses. Be sure to check out the daily specials, which are usually extraordinary. The salads are large enough for a light meal, but be sure to leave room for dessert, especially the decadent chocolate gâteau. *625 W. 5th Ave., tel. 907/276–3546. AE, MC, V.*

$$-$$$ **Simon & Seaforts Saloon and Grill.** This is the place to enjoy a great view across Cook Inlet while dining on consistently fine Alaskan seafood or rock salt-roasted prime rib. The bar is a good spot for appetizers, including beer-batter halibut and potatoes gorgonzola, but you can also order from the full menu. *Corner of 4th Ave. and L St., tel. 907/274–3502. AE, MC, V.*

$–$$ **Thai Cuisine Too.** The menu here is a welcome change from Alaska's ubiquitous seafood and steak houses; you'll find all the Thai standards on the menu, including fresh rolls, Pad-Thai, and a wonderful Tom Khar Gai soup. The food is dependably good, and the atmosphere is quiet. Thai Cuisine Too is right in the center of town and is especially popular for lunch. *328 G St., tel. 907/277–8424. AE, MC, V.*

Brew Pubs

Brew pubs, along with a multitude of espresso stands, have arrived in Anchorage. For visitors limited to touring the city by foot, the downtown area has several breweries/restaurants within easy walking distance from downtown hotels:

Alaska Glacier Brew House Restaurant. Tasty food, such as wood-fired pizza, fresh seafood, and rotisserie-grilled meats, complement the home-brewed beer in a stylish setting with high ceilings and a central fireplace. *737 W. 5th Ave., tel. 907/274–2739. AE, MC, V.*

Humpy's Great Alaskan Alehouse. This immensely popular restaurant and bar has more than 40 draught beers on tap, and cranks out huge plates of halibut tacos, health-nut chicken, and smoked-salmon Caesar salad. Humpy's has live music most evenings, so don't expect quiet (or a smoke-free atmosphere) in this hopping nightspot. *610 W. 6th Ave., tel. 907/276–2337. AE, D, DC, MC, V.*

Railway Brewing Company. The historic Alaska Railroad depot provides a trackside setting for train buffs and beer enthusiasts alike. Sandwiches, burgers, pizzas, and pastas are the mainstays of the menu. A small deck is opened in the summer months for those who want to enjoy the midnight sun. Brewery tours are available. *421 W. 1st Ave., tel. 907/277–1996. AE, D, MC, V.*

Snowgoose Restaurant and Sleeping Lady Brewing Company. The latest addition to the Anchorage brew-pub scene stands out for its large deck with a view of Cook Inlet, Mt. Susitna (the Sleeping Lady), and—on a clear day—Mt. McKinley. The menu includes burgers and pasta, along with seafood specials each evening. Unfortunately, smoke from the upstairs pub (where cigars are allowed) sometimes drifts down to patrons below. *717 W. 3rd Ave., tel. 907/277–7727. AE, MC, V.*

Glacier Bay National Park and Preserve

Cruising Glacier Bay is like revisiting the Little Ice Age, when glaciers covered much of the Northern Hemisphere. This is one of the few places in the world where you can get within a ¼ mi (½ km) of tidewater glaciers, which have their base at the water's edge. Twelve of them line the 60 mi (96 km) of narrow fjords at the northern end of the Inside Passage. Huge chunks of ice break off the glaciers and crash into the water, producing a dazzling show known as calving.

Although the Tlingit Indians have lived in the area for 10,000 years, the bay was first popularized by naturalist John Muir, who visited in 1879. Just 100 years before, the bay was completely choked with ice. By 1916, though, the ice had retreated 65 mi (105 km)—the most rapid glacial retreat ever recorded. To preserve its clues to the world's geological history, Glacier Bay was declared a national monument in 1925. It became a national park in 1980. Today, several of the glaciers in the west arm are advancing again, but very slowly.

Competition is fierce among cruise ships for entry permits into Glacier Bay. To protect the humpback whale, which feeds here in summer, the Park Service limits the number of ships that can call. Check your cruise brochure to make

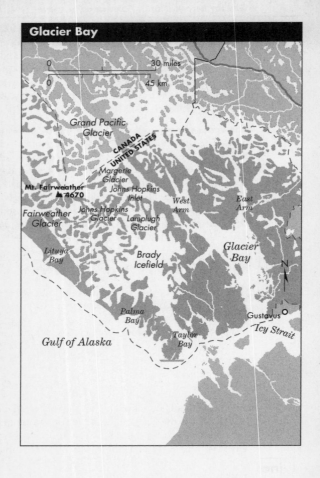

Glacier Bay

0 — 30 miles
0 — 45 km

Grand Pacific Glacier

CANADA
UNITED STATES

Margerie Glacier
Johns Hopkins Inlet

Mt. Fairweather ▲ 4670

Johns Hopkins Glacier
Lamplugh Glacier

West Arm

East Arm

Fairweather Glacier

Brady Icefield

Glacier Bay

Lituya Bay

N

Palma Bay

Gustavus O

Taylor Bay

Icy Strait

Gulf of Alaska

sure that Glacier Bay is included in your sailing. Most
ships that do visit spend at least one full day exploring the
park. There are no shore excursions or landings in the bay,
but a Park Service naturalist boards every cruise ship to provide narration on its history and scientific importance. It
is often misty or rainy, so rain gear is essential. The average summer temperature is 50° F. As always in Alaska, be
prepared for the cold. Also, be sure to bring binoculars, extra
film, and a telephoto lens.

The glaciers that most cruise passengers see are in the west
arm of Glacier Bay. Ships linger in front of five glaciers so
passengers may view their stunning appearance. Most ships
stop briefly at **Reid Glacier** before continuing on to **Lamplugh Glacier**—one of the bluest in the park—at the mouth
of Johns Hopkins Inlet. Next is **Johns Hopkins Glacier** at
the end of the inlet, where cruise passengers are likely to
see a continuous shower of calving ice. Sometimes there are
so many icebergs in the inlet that ships must avoid the area.
Moving farther north, to the end of the western arm, **Margerie Glacier** is also quite active. Adjacent is **Grand Pacific
Glacier,** the largest glacier in the park.

Your experience in Glacier Bay will depend partly on the
size of your ship. Ocean liners tend to stay midchannel, while
small yachtlike ships spend more time closer to shore. Passengers on smaller ships may get a better view of the calving ice and wildlife—such as brown and black bears,
mountain goats, moose, and seals with their pups—but big-
ship passengers, on vessels with much higher decks, get a
loftier perspective. Both types of vessels come within ¼ mi
(½ km) of the glaciers themselves.

Haines

Unlike most other cities in Southeast Alaska, Haines can
be reached by road; the 152-mi (245-km) Haines Highway
connects at Haines Junction with the Alaska Highway.
Missionary S. Hall Young and famed naturalist John Muir
picked the site for this town in 1879 as a place to bring Chris-
tianity and education to the natives. They could hardly have
picked a more beautiful spot. The town sits on a heavily
wooded peninsula with magnificent views of Portage Cove

and the Coastal Mountain Range. It lies 80 mi (129 km) north of Juneau via fjordlike Lynn Canal.

The town has two distinct personalities. On the north side of the Haines Highway is the portion of Haines founded by Young and Muir. After its missionary beginnings the town served as the trailhead for the Jack Dalton Trail to the Yukon during the 1897 gold rush to the Klondike. The following year, when gold was discovered in nearby Porcupine (now deserted), the booming community served as a supply center and jumping-off place for those goldfields as well. Today things are quieter; the town's streets are orderly, its homes are well kept, and for the most part it looks a great deal like any other Alaska seacoast community.

South of the highway, the town looks like a military post, which is what it was for nearly half a century. In 1903 the U.S. Army established a post—Ft. William Henry Seward— at Portage Cove just south of town. For 17 years (1922– 39) the post (renamed Chilkoot Barracks to avoid confusion with the city of Seward, farther north in the southcentral part of the state) was the only military base in the territory. That changed with World War II, when the army built both the Alaska Highway and the Haines Highway to link Alaska with the other states.

After the war, the post closed down, and a group of veterans purchased the property from the government. They changed its name to Port Chilkoot and created residences, businesses, and a Native American arts center from the officers' houses and military buildings that surrounded the old fort's parade ground. Eventually Port Chilkoot merged with the city of Haines. Although the two areas are now officially one municipality, the old military post with its grassy parade ground is referred to as Ft. Seward.

The Haines–Ft. Seward community today is recognized for the Native American dance and culture center at Ft. Seward, as well as for the superb fishing, camping, and outdoor recreation at Chilkoot Lake, Portage Cove, Mosquito Lake, and Chilkat State Park on the shores of Chilkat Inlet. The last locale, one of the small treasures of the Alaska state park system, features views of the Davidson and Rainbow glaciers across the water.

Shore Excursions

The following are good choices in Haines. They may not be offered by all cruise lines. All times and prices are approximate.

ADVENTURE

Glacier Bay Flightseeing. If your cruise doesn't include a visit to Glacier Bay, here's a chance to see several of its tidewater glaciers during a low-altitude flight. *1-hr flight plus transfers. Cost: $125.*

Mountain Biking. Ride through historic Ft. William Henry Seward and view the impressive architecture of this turn-of-the-century U.S. army facility. After the fort, the guide will lead riders through the natural beauty of the Chilkat River estuary. Bikes and equipment are included. *2 hrs. Cost: $45.*

CITY SIGHTS

Haines Cultural and Natural Wonders Tour. This excursion tours Ft. Seward, the Sheldon Museum and Cultural Center, and the Alaska Indian Arts Center and includes time to browse through the downtown galleries. *2½–3 hrs. Cost: $40.*

NATIVE CULTURAL

Chilkat Dancers. A drive through Ft. William Henry Seward includes a dance performance by the Chilkat Dancers, noted for their vivid tribal masks, and a stop at the American Bald Eagle Interpretive Center. Some lines combine this tour with a salmon bake (*see below*). *3 hrs, including 1-hr performance. Cost: $41.*

SALMON BAKE

Chilkat Dancers and Salmon Bake. The narrated tour of Haines and Ft. Seward and a Chilkat Dancers performance are combined with a dinner of salmon grilled over an open fire. *2½–3 hrs. Cost: $55.*

WILDLIFE UP CLOSE

Chilkat River by Jet Boat. A cruise through the Chilkat Bald Eagle Preserve reveals some eagles and—if you're lucky—perhaps a moose or a bear. It is a smooth, rather scenic trip, but in summer, you'll see little wildlife. Come October, though, imagine the trees filled with thousands of bald eagles. *3½ hrs. Cost: $80.*

Coming Ashore

Cruise ships dock in front of Ft. Seward, and downtown Haines is just a short walk away (about ¾ mi). You can pick up walking-tour maps of both Haines and Ft. Seward at the visitor center on 2nd Avenue (tel. 907/766–2234 or 800/458–3579). Most cruise lines provide a complimentary shuttle service to downtown. Taxis are always standing by; hour-long taxi tours of the town cost $10 per person. A one-way trip between the pier and town costs $5. If you need to call for a pickup, contact **The Other Guys Taxi** (tel. 907/766–3257) or **Haines Taxi** (tel. 907/766–3138).

Exploring Haines

Numbers in the margin correspond to points of interest on the Haines map.

❶ The **Sheldon Museum and Cultural Center,** near the foot of Main Street, houses Native American artifacts—including famed Chilkat blankets—plus gold-rush memorabilia such as Jack Dalton's sawed-off shotgun. *25 Main St., tel. 907/766–2366. Admission: $3. Open daily 1–5 and whenever cruise ships are in port.*

❷ The building that houses **Chilkat Center for the Arts** was once Ft. Seward's recreation hall, but now it's the space for Chilkat Indian dancing. Some performances may be at the tribal house next door; check posted notices for performance times. *Ft. Seward, tel. 907/766–2160. Admission: $10. Performances scheduled when cruise ships are in port.*

❸ At **Alaska Indian Arts,** a nonprofit organization dedicated to the revival of Tlingit Indian art forms, you'll see Native carvers making totems, metalsmiths working in silver, and weavers making blankets. *Between Chilkat Center for the Arts and Haines parade ground, tel. 907/766–2160. Admission free. Open weekdays 9–noon and 1–5, and whenever cruise ships are in port.*

Celebrating Haines's location in the "Valley of the Eagles"
❹ is the **American Bald Eagle Foundation Natural History Museum.** The name is a bit too grandiose for this collection of stuffed eagles and other dead animals. A video documents the annual "Gathering of the Eagles," when thousands of (live) bald eagles converge on the Chilkat Bald Eagle Preserve just north of town (*see* Shore Excursions,

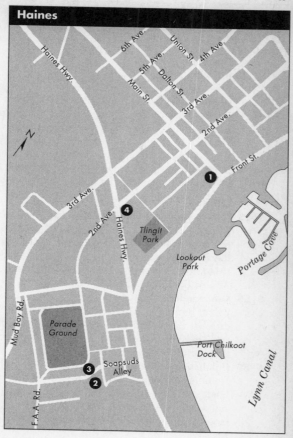

Haines

Alaska Indian
Arts, **3**

American
Bald Eagle
Foundation
National
History
Museum, **4**

Chilkat Center
for the Arts, **2**

Sheldon
Museum and
Cultural
Center, **1**

above). 2nd Ave. and Haines Hwy., tel. 907/766–3094. Admission free; donations accepted. Open when cruise ships are in port.

Sports

HIKING

One of the most rewarding hikes in the area is to the north summit of **Mt. Ripinsky,** the prominent peak that rises 3,610 ft behind the town. Be warned: It's a strenuous trek and requires a full day, so most cruise passengers will want to only try a partial summit. (Make sure you leave plenty of time to get back to your ship.) The trailhead lies at the top of Young Street, along a pipeline right-of-way. For other hikes, pick up a copy of "Haines Is for Hikers" at the visitor center.

Dining

$–$$ **Chilkat Restaurant and Bakery.** Family-style cooking is served in a homelike, no-smoking setting with lace curtains. Seafood, steaks, and sandwiches are cooked to order; Friday is all-you-can-eat night. The bakery has tasty pastries to go. *5th Ave. near Main St., tel. 907/766–2920. AE, MC, V. Closed Sun., winter hrs vary.*

$–$$ **Commander's Room.** Stop here for fresh seafood, fish and chips, burgers, and more. Facing Ft. Seward's parade ground, this restaurant in Hotel Halsingland is a good place to soak up atmosphere. *At Ft. Seward, tel. 907/766–2000 or 800/542–6363. AE, DC, MC, V.*

$–$$ **Lighthouse Restaurant.** You get a great view of Lynn Canal from this restaurant at the foot of Main Street next to the boat harbor. Steaks, seafood, and barbecued ribs are the standards here. Save room for a slice of their famous buttermilk pie. *Front St. on the harbor, tel. 907/766–2442. AE, MC, V.*

$ **Mountain Market & Deli.** This spot is a bit out of the way, but it's a great place to have a mocha or latte and get in synch with Haines's outdoorsy-artist crowd. The fare includes fresh baked goods, soups, and sandwiches. *3rd Ave. at Haines Hwy., tel. 907/766–3340. MC, V.*

Saloons

Harbor Bar (Front St. at the Harbor, tel. 907/766–2444). Commercial fishermen gather nightly at this circa 1907 bar next to the Lighthouse Restaurant. Sometimes there's live music. It's colorful but can get a little loud at night.

Homer

Of the hundreds of thousands of cruise passengers who visit Alaska each year, only a very few get to see Homer. It's a shame. In a state of beautiful places, Homer has emerged as its premier artists colony. Those travelers who do arrive by ship are usually beginning or ending an expedition cruise to the Arctic or traveling aboard an Alaska Marine Highway ferry (*see* Chapter 2). Fortunately, Homer is easily reached from Seward, where all Gulf of Alaska cruises start or finish. If you rent a car, Homer is just 173 mi (278 km) down the Sterling Highway—practically next door by Alaskan standards. Direct bus connections are also available from both Anchorage and Seward; contact **Homer Stage** (tel. 907/272–8644).

The city of Homer lies at the base of a long sandy spit that juts into Kachemak Bay. It was founded just before the turn of the century as a gold-prospecting camp and later became a coal-mining headquarters. Today the town is a funky fishing port with picturesque buildings, good seafood, and beautiful bay views. It's a favorite weekend spot of Anchorage residents who need a change of scene and weather. Halibut fishing is especially good in this area.

Shore Excursions

The following are good choices in Homer. They may not be offered by all cruise lines. All times and prices are approximate.

Above the Spit. See the sights from a flightseeing plane, including nearby Seldovia. Longer flights visit area glaciers; other tours may focus on wildlife spotting. *1 hr. Cost: $145.*

Sights of the Spit. See the unique Homer Spit from the ground, as well as other area sights and attractions. *3 hrs. Cost: $45.*

Wildlife-Watching. Board a local boat for Halibut Cove, Seldovia, or the nearby seabird colonies. *1½ hrs. Cost: $35–$47.*

Coming Ashore

Cruise ships dock at the Homer Spit. Fishing charters, restaurants, and shops line the spit, or passengers can take a taxi to town, where local galleries and additional dining are found. Look for **Day Breeze Shuttle and Tours** (tel. 907/399–1168), which charges $2 per person to the main drag. For door-to-door service, call **Chuck's Cab** (tel. 907/235–2489). A ride from the spit into town will set you back $14 one-way for the first person and $1 for each additional passenger. Taxi tours of Homer are available for around $35 an hour.

Exploring Homer

For an introduction to Homer's history, visit the **Pratt Museum** with three saltwater aquariums and exhibits on pioneers, Native Americans, and the 1989 Prince William Sound oil spill. Outside is a wildflower garden and a ⅓-mi (½-km) nature trail. The museum also leads 1½-hour walking tours of the harbor for $10 per person. *Bartlett St., just off Pioneer Ave., tel. 907/235–8635. Admission: $4. Open daily 10–6.*

Kachemak Bay abounds in wildlife. Shore excursions or local tour operators take visitors to bird rookeries in the bay or across the bay to gravel beaches for clam digging. Many Homer visitors come to fish for salmon or halibut. Most fishing charters will include an opportunity to view whales, seals, sea otters, porpoises, and seabirds close-up. A walk along the docks on Homer Spit at the end of the day is a pleasant chance to watch commercial fishing boats and charter boats unload their catch. The bay supports a large population of puffins and eagles.

Directly across Kachemak Bay from the end of the Homer spit, **Halibut Cove** is a small community of people who make their living on the bay or by selling handicrafts. The Central Charter (tel. 907/235–7847 or 800/478–7847) booking agency runs frequent boats to the cove from Homer. Halibut Cove has an art gallery and a restaurant that serves local seafood. The cove itself is lovely, especially during salmon runs, when fish leap and splash in the clear water. There are also several lodges on this side of the bay, on pristine coves away from summer crowds.

Seldovia, isolated across the bay from Homer, retains the charm of an earlier Alaska. The town's Russian bloodline shows through in its onion-dome church and its name, derived from a Russian place-name meaning "herring bay."

Those who fish use plenty of herring for bait, catching salmon, halibut, and king or Dungeness crab. You'll find excellent fishing whether you drop your line into the deep waters of Kachemak Bay or cast into the surf for silver salmon on the shore of Outside Beach, near town. Self-guided hiking or berry picking in late July are other options. Seldovia can be reached from Homer by boat, and the dock of the small boat harbor is in the center of town—allowing for easy exploration. For a guided historical tour, contact South Shore Tours (tel. 907/234–8000).

Shopping

The galleries on and around Pioneer Avenue, including **Ptarmigan Arts** (471 E. Pioneer Ave., tel. 907/235–5345), a local cooperative, are good places to find works by the town's residents. For contemporary art pieces, head to **Bunnell Street Galley** (106 W. Bunnell St., tel. 907/235–2662)—it's next to Two Sisters (*see below*).

Dining

$$$ **Homestead Restaurant.** Eight miles (13 kilometers) from town, this log roadhouse overlooking Kachemak Bay is where locals take guests for a night out. The fare here includes Caesar salads, steak, prime rib, and fresh seafood; the flavors are rich and spicy, with splashes of mango, macadamia nuts, and garlic. *Mile 8.2 East End Rd., tel. 907/235–8723. AE, MC, V. Closed Jan.–Feb.*

$$$ **The Saltry in Halibut Cove.** Exotically prepared local seafood dishes, including curries and pastas, and a wide selection of imported beers are served here. The deck overlooks the boat dock and the cove. It's a good place to while away the afternoon or evening, meandering along the boardwalk and visiting galleries. Dinner seatings are at 6 and 7:30. *Take the* Danny J *ferry ($17.50 round-trip) from Homer harbor; tel. 907/235–7847. Reservations essential. MC, V. Open summer only.*

$ **Café Cups.** With microbrewery beer on tap and local artists' works on the walls, this renovated house offers more than just great food, fresh-baked breads, and desserts. Locals and visitors alike crowd into the cozy dining room for coffee and conversation in the morning or later in the day for fresh pasta, local seafood, and an eclectic but reasonably priced wine selection. Desserts include a triple decadent cheese-

cake and black-bottom almond cream pie. The outside
deck is a fine place to enjoy a lazy morning while savoring
your eggs Florentine. *162 W. Pioneer Ave., tel. 907/235–
8330. MC, V.*

$ **Two Sisters.** For a delightful taste of the real Homer, visit
this tiny coffeehouse-bakery housed in a historic building.
The funky, mixed crowd here includes fishermen, writers,
and local businesspeople drinking perfectly brewed espresso,
talking politics, and sampling pastries that are to die for.
Two Sisters gets crowded on weekend mornings—you'll see
folks overflowing out to the porch. *106 W. Bunnell St., tel.
907/235–2280. No credit cards. No dinner.*

Saloon

Salty Dawg Saloon (tel. 907/235–9990) is famous all over
Alaska. Fishermen, cannery workers, and carpenters have
been holding court here for decades in this friendly and noisy
pub. Today they're joined by college kids working in the
gift shops, retirees, and tourists. Near the end of the spit,
the Salty Dawg is easy to find; just look for the "lighthouse."

Tastes of Alaska

Alaska Wild Berry Products (528 Pioneer Ave., tel. 907/235–
8858 or 800/280–2927) manufactures jams, jellies, sauces,
syrups, chocolate-covered candies, and juices made from
wild berries handpicked on the Kenai Peninsula; shipping
is available. Alaska Wild Berry also has a big confectionery
kitchen and gift shop in Anchorage at 5225 Juneau Street.

Juneau

Juneau owes its origins to a trio of colorful characters: two
pioneers, Joe Juneau and Dick Harris, and a Tlingit chief
named Kowee, who discovered rich reserves of gold in the
stream that now runs through the middle of town. That was
in 1880, and shortly after the discovery a modest stampede
led first to the formation of a camp, then a town, then the
Alaska district (now state) capital.

For nearly 60 years after Juneau's founding, gold remained
the mainstay of the economy. In its heyday, the Alaska
Juneau gold mine was the biggest low-grade-ore mine in
the world. Then, during World War II, the government decided it needed Juneau's manpower for the war effort, and

BONUS MILES MAKE
GREAT SOUVENIRS.

Earn Miles With Your MCI Card.

Take the MCI Card along on this trip and start earning miles for the next one. You'll earn frequent flyer miles on all your calls and save with the low rates you've come to expect from MCI. Before you know it, you'll be on your way to some other international destination.

Sign up for MCI by calling 1-800-FLY-FREE

Is this a great time, or what? :-)

Earn Frequent Flyer Miles.

AmericanAirlines
AAdvantage

Continental Airlines
OnePass

Delta Air Lines
SkyMiles

HAWAIIAN
AIRLINES

MIDWEST EXPRESS
AIRLINES

NORTHWEST
AIRLINES
WORLDPERKS

Rapid Rewards
SOUTHWEST AIRLINES

MILEAGE PLUS
United Airlines

US AIRWAYS
DIVIDEND MILES

With guidebooks for every kind of travel—from weekend getaways to island hopping to adventures abroad—it's easy to understand why smart travelers go with **Fodor's**.

At bookstores everywhere.
www.fodors.com

Smart travelers go with **Fodor's**™

the mines ceased operations. After the war, mining failed to start up again, and the government became the city's principal employer.

Juneau is a charming, cosmopolitan frontier town. It's easy to navigate, has one of the best museums in Alaska, is surrounded by beautiful (and accessible) wilderness, and has a glacier in its backyard. To capture the true frontier ambience, stop by the Red Dog Saloon or the Alaskan Hotel. Both are on the main shopping drag, just a quick walk from the cruise ship pier.

Shore Excursions

The following are good choices in Juneau. They may not be offered by all cruise lines. All times and prices are approximate.

ADVENTURE

Mendenhall Glacier Helicopter Ride. One of the best helicopter glacier tours, including a landing on an ice field for a walk on the glacier. Boots and rain gear provided. *2¼ hrs, including 30-min flight. Cost: $165.*

Mendenhall River Float Trip. A rafting trip down the Mendenhall River passes through some stretches of gentle rapids. Experienced oarsmen row the rafts; rubber boots, ponchos, and life jackets are provided. The minimum age is six. An excellent first rafting experience for those in good health, it's great fun. *3½ hrs. Cost: $80–$100.*

SALMON BAKES

Gold Creek Salmon Bake. This all-you-can-eat outdoor meal includes Alaskan king salmon barbecued over an open alder-wood fire. After dinner, walk in the woods, explore the abandoned mine area, or pan for gold. *1½–2 hrs. Cost: $25–$30.*

Taku Glacier Lodge Flightseeing and Salmon Bake. Fly over the Juneau Ice Field to Taku Glacier Lodge. Dine on barbecued salmon, then explore the virgin rain forest or enjoy the lodge. It's expensive, but this trip consistently gets rave reviews. *3 hrs. Cost: $180–$200.*

Coming Ashore

Most cruise ships dock or tender passengers ashore at **Marine Park** or at the old **Ferry Terminal.** Princess ships (and some others) tie up at the **South Franklin Dock.** Ask aboard your ship exactly which facility you'll be using. Both Marine Park and the Ferry Terminal are within easy walking distance of the downtown shops and attractions. The South Franklin Dock is about a fifth of a mile, or an eight-minute walk, from the edge of downtown and the new Mt. Roberts tram. For those who prefer not to walk, a shuttle bus ($1 round-trip) runs from the dock to town whenever ships are in town.

For visitor information, there's a small kiosk (staffed according to cruise ship arrivals) on the pier at Marine Park filled with tour brochures, bus schedules, and maps. There is a tourist information center at the old ferry terminal as well. The downtown shops along South Franklin Street are just minutes away.

You won't need to hire a taxi in Juneau unless you are heading to the glacier. In that case, taxis will be waiting for you at Marine Park. Another option is the city bus that stops on South Franklin Street. For $1.25, it'll take you within 1¼ mi (3½ km) of the Mendenhall Visitor Center. The **Glacier Express** (tel. 907/789–0052 or 800/478–0052) provides direct bus service between downtown and the glacier for $10 round-trip.

Exploring Juneau
Numbers in the margin correspond to points of interest on the Juneau map.

❶ A block east of the cruise ship docks at Marine Park is **South Franklin Street.** The buildings here and on Front Street, which intersects South Franklin several blocks north, are among the oldest and most interesting in the city. Many reflect the architecture of the 1920s and '30s; some are even older.

At No. 278 South Franklin Street is the **Red Dog Saloon.** With a sawdust-covered floor, a stuffed bear, and big-game heads mounted on the walls, this is Alaska's most famous saloon.

Just down the street from the Red Dog Saloon is the small **Alaskan Hotel** (167 S. Franklin St.), which was called "a pocket edition of the best hotels on the Pacific Coast" when it opened in 1913. Owners Mike and Betty Adams

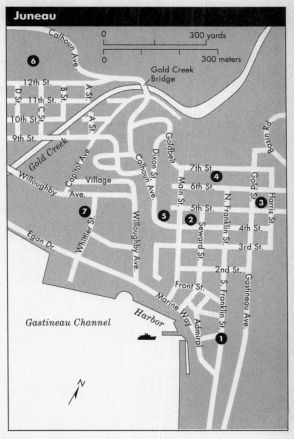

Juneau

0   300 yards
0   300 meters

Gold Creek Bridge

Gastineau Channel

Harbor

Alaska State Capitol, **2**

Alaska State Museum, **7**

City Museum, **5**

Evergreen Cemetery, **6**

House of Wickersham, **4**

St. Nicholas Russian Orthodox Church, **3**

South Franklin Street, **1**

have restored the building with period trappings. The bar-room's massive, mirrored oak bar, accented by Tiffany lamps and panels, is a particular delight.

Also on South Franklin Street is the **Alaska Steam Laundry Building,** a 1901 structure with a windowed turret. It now houses a great collection of photos from Juneau's past, a popular espresso shop (Heritage Coffee Co., tel. 907/586–1752), and several stores.

Across the street from the Steam Laundry Building, the equally venerable **Senate Building Mall** (175 S. Franklin St.) contains one of the two Juneau Christmas stores, a fine jewelry shop, a place to buy Russian icons, and even a shop with goods from Ireland.

❷ At the corner of Seward Street is the **Alaska State Capitol,** constructed in 1930, with pillars of southeastern-Alaska marble. The structure now houses the governor's office and other state agencies, and the state legislature meets here January through May each year. *Tel. 907/465–2479. Tours weekdays 8:30–4:30 in summer. Call for hours of weekend tours.*

❸ At the top of the hill on 5th Street is little **St. Nicholas Russian Orthodox Church,** built in 1894. Here you can see icons that date from the 1700s. *326 5th St., off Gold St., tel. 907/586–1023. Donation requested. Open daily 9–6 in summer.*

❹ The **House of Wickersham,** the 1899 residence of James Wickersham, a pioneer judge and delegate to Congress, houses memorabilia from the judge's travels, ranging from rare Native American basketry and ivory carvings to historic photos, 47 diaries, and a Chickering grand piano that came "round the horn" to Alaska when the Russians still ruled the region. *213 7th St., tel. 907/586–9001. Admission: $2.50. Tours Mon.–Sat. noon–5.*

❺ Two fine totem poles flank the entrance to Juneau's **City Museum.** Inside, the city's history is relayed through memorabilia, gold-mining exhibits, and videos. *4th and Main Sts., tel. 907/586–3572. Admission: $2. Open weekdays 9–5, weekends 10–5.*

❻ **Evergreen Cemetery** is where many Juneau pioneers (including Joe Juneau and Dick Harris) are buried. At the end of the gravel lane is the monument to Chief Kowee, who was cremated on this spot.

❼ The **Alaska State Museum** is one of Alaska's best, with exhibits on the state's history, Native cultures, wildlife, industry, and art. *395 Whittier St., tel. 907/465–2901. Admission: $3. Open weekdays 9–6, weekends 10–6.*

Mendenhall Glacier is only 13 mi (21 km) from downtown, and you can walk right up to it.

For a great view of the harbor, take **Mt. Roberts Tram** (490 S. Franklin St., tel. 907/463–3412 or 800/461–8726) to an observation deck 2,000 ft above Juneau. Walking paths lead from the visitors center (*see* Hiking, *below*), which also has retail shops, a restaurant and bar, a nature center, and an auditorium that shows films on native culture and bears. You can catch the tram from the base terminal downtown—it's within walking distance of the cruise ship piers. For $17.75, you get unlimited rides for the day

Shopping

South Franklin Street is the place in Juneau to shop. The variety of merchandise is good, though some shops offer an abundance of Made-in-China Alaskan keepsakes. You'll pay high prices for authentic native handicrafts or hand-knitted sweaters. One of the better galleries is **Mt. Juneau Artists** (211 Front St., tel. 907/586–2108), an arts and crafts cooperative.

In the Senate Building Mall on South Franklin Street is the **Russian Shop** (tel. 907/586–2778), a repository of icons, samovars, lacquered boxes, nesting dolls, and other items that reflect Alaska's 18th- and 19th-century Russian heritage.

For a souvenir from one of Alaska's most famous saloons, stop by the gift shop at the **Red Dog Saloon** (*see* Exploring Juneau, *above*).

Knowledgeable locals frequent the **Rie Munoz Gallery** (2101 N. Jordon Ave., tel. 907/789–7411) for fine art. Munoz is one of Alaska's favorite artists, and her stylized, colorful design technique is much copied. Other artists' works are also on sale, including woodblock prints by nationally known artist Dale DeArmond. Another fun place to browse is the **Wm. Spear Designs Gallery** (165 S. Franklin St., tel.

907/586–2209). His colorful enameled pins are witty, creative, amusing, and sometimes simply perverse.

Sports

FISHING

More than 30 charter boat operators offer fishing trips in the Juneau area; stop by the **Davis Log Cabin** (3rd and Seward Sts., tel. 907/586–2201) for a complete listing.

HIKING

Surrounded by the **Tongass National Forest,** Juneau is a hiker's paradise. For trail maps, information, and advice, stop by Centennial Hall on Willoughby at Egan Drive (tel. 907/586–8751).

The Davis Log Cabin (3rd and Seward Sts., tel. 907/586–2201) sells two useful booklets, "90 Short Walks Around Juneau" ($5) and "Juneau Trails" ($4). Good trails for cruise passengers begin just behind the **Mendenhall Glacier Visitor Center** (*see* Exploring Juneau, *above*).

For guided walks, the **Juneau Parks and Recreation Department** (tel. 907/586–5226) sponsors Wednesday- and Saturday-morning group hikes. On Saturday, there's free car-pool pickup at the docks.

Gastineau Guiding (tel. 907/586–2666) leads guided hikes from the nature center at the top of Mt. Roberts Tram. A one-hour hike costs $30 including the tram ride; a four-hour hike costs $50.

KAYAKING

Alaska Discovery (tel. 907/780–6226 or 800/586–1911) offers escorted day tours for $95 per person. Lunch and rain gear are included. Trips leave around 9:30 AM and return about 5 PM, so participation is practical only for passengers whose ships make day-long calls.

Dining

$–$$$ **Fiddlehead Restaurant and Bakery.** Definitely a favorite with Juneau locals, this delightful place decorated with light wood, stained glass, and historic photos, serves generous portions of healthy fare. How about a light dinner of black beans and rice? Or pasta Greta Garbo (locally smoked salmon tossed with fettuccine in cream sauce). Their bakery always has delicious breads, croissants, and sweets.

Upstairs, the Fireweed Room features a more diverse menu, along with folk and jazz music most nights. *429 W. Willoughby Ave., tel. 907/586–3150. AE, D, DC, MC, V.*

$ **Armadillo Tex-Mex Cafe.** A devoted clientele of locals wait in line to order border eats at this bustling, boisterous café. Check the daily specials, or if you aren't too hungry, order a big bowl of homemade chili and cornbread. *431 S. Franklin St., tel. 907/586–1880. MC, V.*

Saloons

Juneau is one of the best saloon towns in all of Alaska. Try stopping in one of the following:

Alaskan Hotel Bar (167 S. Franklin St., tel. 907/586–1000). This spot is popular with locals and is distinctly less touristy. If live music isn't playing, an old-fashioned player piano usually is.

Bubble Room (127 N. Franklin St., tel. 907/586–2660). This comfortable lounge off the lobby in the Baranof Hotel is quiet—and the site (so it is said) of more legislative lobbying and decision making than in the nearby state capitol building. The music from the piano bar is soft.

Red Dog Saloon (278 S. Franklin St., tel. 907/463–3777). This pub carries on the sawdust-on-the-floor tradition, with a mounted bear and other game animal trophies on the walls and lots of historic photos. There's live music, and the crowd is raucous, particularly when cruise ships are in port.

Tastes of Alaska

When you're "shopping" the bars and watering holes of Southeast Alaska, ask for Alaskan Amber, Frontier Beer, or Pale Ale. All are brewed and bottled in Juneau. If you'd like to see how this award-winning brew is crafted, visit the **Alaskan Brewing Company.** *5429 Shaune Dr., Juneau, tel. 907/780–5866. Open Tues.–Sat. 11–4:30.*

Kenai Peninsula

Salmon fishing, scenery, and wildlife are the standouts of the Kenai Peninsula, which thrusts into the Gulf of Alaska south of Anchorage. Commercial fishing is important to the area's economy, and the city of Kenai, on the peninsula's northwest coast, is the base for the Cook Inlet offshore oil fields.

The area is dotted with roadside campgrounds, and you can explore three major federal holdings on the peninsula—the western end of the sprawling **Chugach National Forest,** along with **Kenai National Wildlife Refuge,** and **Kenai Fjords National Park.**

Portage Glacier, 50 mi (80 km) southeast of Anchorage, is one of Alaska's most frequently visited tourist destinations. A 6-mi (10-km) side road off the Seward Highway leads to the Begich-Boggs Visitor Center (tel. 907/783–2326) on the shore of Portage Lake. The center houses impressive displays that will tell you all you need to know about glaciers. Boat tours of the face of the glacier are conducted aboard the 200-passenger *Ptarmigan.* Unfortunately, the glacier is receding rapidly, and is no longer pushing so many icebergs into the lake, so the views are not what they once were.

The mountains surrounding Portage Glacier are covered with smaller glaciers. A short hike to Byron Glacier Overlook, about a mile (1½ km) west, is popular in the spring and summer. Twice weekly in summer, naturalists lead free treks in search of microscopic ice worms. Keep an eye out for black bears in all the Portage side valleys in the summer.

Ketchikan

At the base of 3,000-ft Deer Mountain, Ketchikan is the definitive Southeast Alaska town. Houses cling to the steep hillsides and the harbors are filled with fishing boats. Until miners and fishermen settled here in the 1880s, the mouth of Ketchikan Creek was a summer fishing camp for Tlingit Indians. Today the town runs on fishing, tourism, and logging.

Ketchikan is Alaska's totem-pole port: At the nearby Tlingit village of Saxman, 2½ mi (5 km) south of downtown, there is a major totem park, and residents still practice traditional carving techniques. The Ketchikan Visitors Bureau on the dock can supply information on getting to Saxman on your own, or you can take a ship-organized tour. Another excellent outdoor totem display is at Totem Bight

State Historical Park, a coastal rain forest 10 mi (16 km) north of town. The Totem Heritage Center preserves historic poles, some nearly 200 years old.

Expect rain at some time during the day, even if the sun is shining when you dock: Average annual precipitation is more than 150 inches.

Shore Excursions

The following are good choices in Ketchikan. They may not be offered by all cruise lines. All times and prices are approximate.

ADVENTURE

Misty Fjords Flightseeing. Aerial views of granite cliffs rising 4,000 ft from the sea, waterfalls, rain forests, and wildlife lead to a landing on a high wilderness lake. *2 hrs, including 65-min flight. Cost: $155–$180.*

Sportfishing. You're almost sure to get a bite in the "Salmon Capital of the World." Charter boats hold up to 16 passengers; fish can be butchered and shipped home for an additional charge. *4–5 hrs, including 3–4 hrs of fishing. Cost: $160.*

NATIVE CULTURE

Saxman Village. See 27 totem poles and totem carvers at work at this Native community. The gift shop is among the best for Alaska Native crafts. *2½ hrs. Cost: $45.*

Totem Bight Tour. This look at Ketchikan's native culture focuses on Tlingit totem poles in Totem Bight State Historical Park. Guides interpret the myths and symbols in the traditional carvings. *2½ hrs. Cost: $30.*

Coming Ashore

Ships dock or tender passengers ashore directly across from the Ketchikan Visitors Bureau on Front and Mission streets, in the center of downtown. Here you can pick up brochures and maps.

The impressive **Southeast Alaska Visitor Center** has exhibits on native culture, wildlife, logging, recreation, and the use of public lands. You can also watch their award-winning film, "Mystical Southeast Alaska." *50 Main St., tel. 907/228–6214. Admission: $4.*

Ketchikan is easy to explore, with walking-tour signs to lead you around the city. Most of the town's sights are within easy walking distance. A new paved bike-and-foot path leads to the city of Saxman, for those who wish to walk to the Native village—but remember it's 2½ mi (5 km) from downtown Ketchikan.

To reach the sights outside downtown on your own, you'll want to hire a cab or ride the local buses. Metered taxis meet the ships right on the docks and also wait across the street. Rates are $2.10 for pickup, 23¢ each ⅒ mi.

Exploring Ketchikan

Numbers in the margin correspond to points of interest on the Ketchikan map.

❶ You can learn about Ketchikan's early days of fishing, mining, and logging at the **Tongass Historical Museum and Totem Pole.** *In the library building at Dock and Bawden Sts., tel. 907/225–5600. Admission: $2. Open daily 8–5 in summer.*

❷ For a great view of the harbor, take curving Venetia Avenue to the **Westmark Cape Fox Lodge.** Not only are the views stunning at the lodge, but the dining is excellent. You can also take a tramway ride ($1) down the mountainside to popular Creek Street (*see below*).

❸ Every visitor to Ketchikan should stop by the **Totem Heritage Center,** which has a fascinating display of weathered, original totem carvings. *Woodland Ave. at corner of Deermont St., tel. 907/225–5900. Admission: $4. Open daily 8–5 during cruise season.*

❹ **Creek Street,** formerly Ketchikan's infamous red-light district, remains the picturesque centerpiece of town. Its small houses, built on stilts over the creek, have been restored as trendy shops. The street's most famous brothel, **Dolly's House** (tel. 907/225–5900, admission: $3.50), has been preserved as a museum, complete with original furnishings and a short history of the life and times of Ketchikan's best-known madam. There's good salmon viewing in season at the Creek Street footbridge. You can catch the tram here for a ride up to the Westmark Cape Fox Lodge, if you missed it before (*see above*).

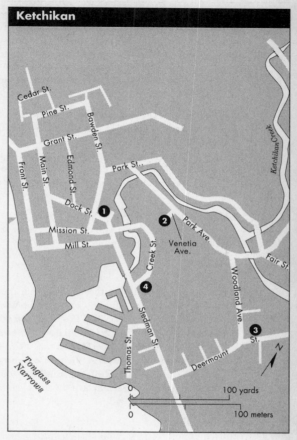

Ketchikan

Cedar St.
Pine St.
Bawden St.
Grant St.
Front St.
Main St.
Edmond St.
Park St.
Dock St.
1
Mission St.
2
Park Ave.
Mill St.
Venetia Ave.
Creek St.
Ketchikan Creek
Fair St.
Woodland Ave.
4
Thomas St.
Stedman St.
3
St.
Deermount
Tongass Narrows
N

100 yards

100 meters

0

0

Creek Street, **4**

Tongass Historical Museum and Totem Pole, **1**

Totem Heritage Center, **3**

Westmark Cape Fox Lodge, **2**

Shopping

Because artists are local, prices for Native American crafts are better in Ketchikan than at most other ports. The **Saxman Village** gift shop has some Tlingit merchandise, along with less expensive mass-produced souvenirs. A better bet is to head a block downhill to **Saxman Arts Co-op** (tel. 907/225–4166) where the crafts are all locally made.

Creek Street has several attractive boutiques. At **Parnassus Bookstore** (5 Creek St., tel. 907/225–7690), you can browse through an eclectic collection of books. The same building houses two fine arts and crafts shops: **Alaska Eagle Arts** (tel. 907/225–8365) and **Soho Coho** (tel. 907/225–5954). The latter is headquarters for artist Ray Troll, Alaska's famed producer of all things weird and fishy.

Salmon, Etc. (322 Mission St., tel. 907/225–6008) sells every variety of Alaskan salmon, which can be sent, frozen and processed, to your home.

Sports

FISHING

Salmon are so plentiful in these waters that the town has earned the nickname "Salmon Capital of the World." Contact **Chinook Charters** (tel. 907/225–9225), **Ketchikan Charter Boats** (tel. 907/225–7291), **Chip Port Charters** (tel. 907/225–2447), or **Knudson Cove Marina** (tel. 907/247–8500). The **Ketchikan Convention & Visitors Bureau** (tel. 907/225–6166 or 800/770–2200) has a full list of other charter companies; they will send you a vacation planner as well.

HIKING

Check at the visitors bureau on the dock for trail maps and advice. If you're a tough hiker with sturdy shoes, the trail from downtown (starting at the end of Fair Street) to the top of **Deer Mountain** will repay your effort with a spectacular panorama of the city below and the wilderness behind. It's 6 mi (10 km) round-trip. The **Ward Lake Area,** about 6 mi (10 km) north of town, offers easier hiking along lakes and streams and beneath towering spruce and hemlock trees.

The Southeast Alaska Visitor Center (*see* Coming Ashore, *above*) has trail maps detailing these and other U.S. Forest Service trails.

Both **Southeast Exposure** (507 Stedman St., tel. 907/225–8829) and **Southeast Sea Kayaks** (tel. 907/225–1258) offer sea kayak rentals, instruction, and tours. Three-hour tours (all gear included) cost around $70.

Dining

$$–$$$ **Annabelle's Keg and Chowder House.** In the Gilmore Hotel, this seafood restaurant takes you back to the 1920s. The walls are covered with photos and paintings depicting the Ketchikan of years past. Specials include steamers, oysters on the half shell, delicious clam chowder, steaks, and pasta. Afterwards, be sure to order a slice of peanut butter pie. *326 Front St., tel. 907/225–6009. AE, D, DC, MC, V.*

$ **Five Star Cafe.** One of Creek Street's old bordellos is now a trendy café serving espresso coffees and an earthy selection of breakfast and lunch choices—sandwiches, soups, salads, pastries—that are always well-prepared. This is where you'll meet young Ketchikan business folk and post-hippie funksters. *5 Creek St., tel. 907/247–7827. No credit cards.*

Saloons

Annabelle's Keg and Chowder House (326 Front St., tel. 907/225–6009). This restaurant-lounge with a jukebox in the Gilmore Hotel blends old and new Alaska in a semi-formal atmosphere. There's no pretense of formality at the **Potlatch Bar** (tel. 907/225–4855) in Thomas Basin, where local fishermen and cannery workers play pool and tip back cans of Rainier Beer.

Misty Fjords National Monument

In the past, cruise ships used to bypass Misty Fjords on their way up and down the Inside Passage. But today more and more cruise passengers are discovering its unspoiled beauty. Ships big and small, from the yachtlike vessels of Alaska Sightseeing to the liners of Crystal, Cunard, Norwegian Cruise Line, and others, now feature a day of scenic cruising through this protected wilderness. At the southern end of the Inside Passage, Misty Fjords usually lies just before or after a call at Ketchikan. The attraction here is the wilderness—3,500 square mi of it—highlighted by waterfalls and cliffs that rise 3,000 ft.

Petersburg

Getting to Petersburg is an experience. Only ferries and the smallest cruise ships can squeak through Wrangell Narrows with the aid of more than 50 buoys and markers along the 22-mi (35-km) crossing. At times the channel seems too narrow for ships to pass through, making for a nail-biting—though safe—trip. The inaccessibility of Petersburg is part of its off-the-beaten-path charm. Unlike at several other Southeast communities, you'll never be overwhelmed by the hordes of cruise passengers here.

At first sight of Petersburg you may think you're in the old country. Neat, white, Scandinavian-style homes and storefronts with steep roofs and bright-colored swirls of leaf and flower designs (called rosemaling) and row upon row of sturdy fishing vessels in the harbor invoke the spirit of Norway. No wonder. This prosperous fishing community was founded by Norwegian Peter Buschmann in 1897.

The Little Norway Festival is held here each year on the third full weekend in May. If you're in town during the festival, be sure to partake in one of the fish feeds that highlight the Norwegian Independence Day celebration. The beer-batter halibut is delectable, and you won't find better folk dancing outside of Norway.

Shore Excursions

The following are good choices in Petersburg. They may not be offered by all cruise lines. All times and prices are approximate.

ADVENTURE

LeConte Flightseeing. One of the best flightseeing tours in Alaska takes you to the southernmost calving glacier in North America. *45-min flight. Cost: $123.*

Petersburg by Bus. Here's a chance to get outside of town and see the scenery. The tour also includes Norwegian refreshments and a performance of Norwegian dance at the Sons of Norway Hall. *2 hrs. Cost: $26.*

Walking Tour. A guide will relate the history and fishing heritage of Petersburg as you explore the old part of town on foot. *1½ hrs. Cost: $10.*

Coming Ashore

Ships small enough to visit Petersburg dock in the South Harbor, which is about a ½-mi (1-km) walk to downtown. Everything in Petersburg is within easy walking distance of the harbor. Renting a bicycle is an especially pleasant way to see the sights. A good route is to ride along the coast on Nordic Drive, past the lovely homes, to the boardwalk and the city dump, where you might spot some bears. Coming back to town, take the interior route and you'll pass the airport and some pretty churches before returning to the waterfront. Bicycles are available for rent from **Northern Bikes** (110 N. Nordic Dr., tel. 907/772–3978) at the Scandia House Hotel.

Passengers who want to learn about the local history, the commercial fishing industry, and the natural history of the Tongass National Forest can book a guided van tour. Contact **See Alaska Tours and Charters** (tel. 907/772–4656).

Exploring Petersburg

Numbers in the margin correspond to points of interest on the Petersburg map.

One of the most pleasant things to do in Petersburg is to roam among the fishing vessels tied up at dockside. This is one of Alaska's busiest, most prosperous fishing communities, and the variety of seacraft is enormous. You'll see small trollers, big halibut vessels, and sleek pleasure craft as well. Wander, too, around the fish-processing structures (though beware of the pungent aroma). Just by watching shrimp, salmon, or halibut catches being brought ashore, you can get a real appreciation for this industry and the people who engage in it.

Overlooking the city harbor there are great viewing and picture-taking vantage points. The peaks of the Coastal Range behind the town mark the border between Canada and the United States; the most striking is **Devils Thumb** at 9,077 ft (2,767 m). About 25 mi (40 km) east of Petersburg lies spectacular **LeConte Glacier,** the continent's southernmost tidewater glacier and one of its most active. Oftentimes so many icebergs have calved into the bay that the entrance is carpeted bank-to-bank with floating bergs. The glacier is accessible only by water or air.

For a scenic hike closer to town, go north on Nordic Drive
① to **Sandy Beach,** where there's frequently good eagle viewing and access to one of Petersburg's favorite picnic and
recreation locales.

The best place to watch for America's national bird is the
② appropriately named **Eagle's Roost Park,** along the shore
north of the Petersburg Fisheries cannery. At low tide you
may see more than two dozen eagles here.

Still another photo opportunity lies in the center of town
③ at **Hammer Slough,** where houses built on stilts make for
a postcard-perfect picture. The large, white, barnlike struc-
④ ture on stilts that borders the slough is the **Sons of Norway
Hall,** where locals work to keep alive the traditions and culture from the old country.

Those wanting to do some sightseeing in town should head
⑤ northeast up the hill from the visitor center to the **Clausen
Museum** and the bronze *Fisk* (Norwegian for "fish") sculp-
ture at 2nd and Fram streets. The museum—not surprisingly—devotes a lot of its space to fishing and processing.
There's an old "iron chink," used in the early days for gut-
ting and cleaning fish, as well as displays that illustrate the
workings of several types of fishing boats. A 126½-pound
king salmon, the largest ever caught, came out of a fish trap
on Prince of Wales Island in 1939 and is on exhibit, as is
the world's largest chum salmon—a 36-pounder. Also here
are displays of Native artifacts. *203 Fram St., tel. 907/
772–3598. Admission: $2. Open Mon.–Sat. 10–4, Sun.
1–4 in summer.*

Three **pioneer churches**—Catholic, Lutheran, and Presbyterian—are nearby at Dolphin and 3rd streets, Excel and
5th streets, and on Haugen Street between 2nd and 3rd
streets, respectively. Of the three, the 50-year-old Lutheran
edifice is the oldest. It is said that boys would bring dirt by
the wheelbarrow load for landscaping around the foundation. Their compensation? Ice-cream cones. The entice-
ment was so successful that, after three years of ice-cream
rewards, it was necessary to bring in a bulldozer to scrape
off the excess dirt.

Petersburg

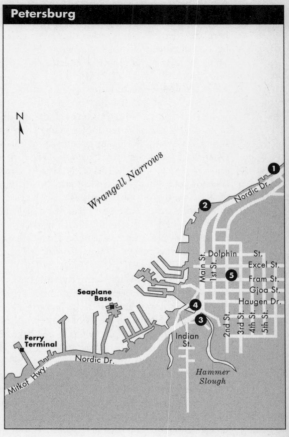

N

Wrangell Narrows

Nordic Dr.

Main St.
1st St.
Dolphin
St.
Excel St.
Fram St.
Gjoa St.
Haugen Dr.

2nd St.
3rd St.
4th St.
5th St.

Seaplane
Base

Ferry
Terminal

Nordic Dr.

Milkof Hwy.

Indian
St.

Hammer
Slough

Clausen
Museum, **5**
Eagle's Roost
Park, **2**
Hammer
Slough, **3**
Sandy Beach, **1**
Sons of
Norway
Hall, **4**

Dining

$–$$ Pellerito's Pizza. The service may be slow, but the pizzas here are great. Recommended toppings include Canadian bacon and pineapple or local shrimp. The bar at Pellerito's pours all sorts of microbrewed beers. *Across from ferry terminal, tel. 907/772–3727. MC, V.*

$ AlasKafe Coffeehouse. Looking for a smoke-free place to hang out? AlasKafe has light meals all day: panini sandwiches, homemade soups, pastas, salads, and desserts. Plus, of course, coffee. The outdoor balcony seats are nice on a sunny day, and on Saturday evenings you'll hear local musicians and poets perform. *Upstairs at the corner of Nordic and Excel, tel. 907/772–5282. No credit cards.*

$ Coastal Cold Storage Fish Market. This is the place to go for fresh seafood in Petersburg. Although primarily a lunch eatery, they are also open for breakfast and dinner, with fish chowders, beer-batter halibut, shrimp cocktail, and sandwiches. They also ship fresh, smoked, canned, or frozen fish, or process any that you catch. *Corner of Excel and Main Sts., tel. 907/772–4171. No credit cards.*

$ Helse. Natural foods, including enormous vegetable-laden sandwiches, are a specialty in this homey cross between a diner and a restaurant. Helse, a favorite lunchtime spot with locals, is filled with plenty of plants and works by local artists. You'll find soups, chowders, home-baked breads, and salads on the menu. Espresso makes a nice ending to a meal. Breakfast consists only of coffee and pastries. *Sing Lee Alley and Harbor Way, tel. 907/772–3444. No credit cards.*

$ The Homestead. There's nothing at all fancy here, just basic American fare: steaks, local prawns, and halibut, a salad bar, and especially generous breakfasts. Rhubarb pie is the fastest-selling item on the menu. This 24-hour joint is popular with chain-smoking locals. *217 Main St., tel. 907/772–3900. DC, MC, V.*

Saloons

Harbor Bar (Nordic Dr. near Dolphin St., tel. 907/772–4526). The name suggests the decor here—ship's wheels, ship pictures, and a mounted red snapper.

Kito's Kave (on Sing Lee Alley, tel. 907/772–3207). A colorful, authentic Alaskan bar of regional fame, Kito's serves Mexican food in a pool-hall atmosphere. It's not for the timid or faint-hearted. Beer drinkers are really better off heading to the bar at Pellerito's Pizza (*see* Dining, *above*), or getting a pitcher of draught from **Harbor Lights Pizza** (tel. 907/772–3424), overlooking the harbor on Sing Lee Alley.

Tastes of Alaska

One of the Southeast's gourmet delicacies is "Petersburg shrimp." Small (they're seldom larger than half your pinky finger), tender, and succulent, they're much treasured by Alaskans, who often send them "outside" as thank-you gifts. You'll find the little critters fresh in meat departments and canned in gift sections at food stores throughout the Panhandle. You can buy fresh vacuum-packed Petersburg shrimp in Petersburg at **Coastal Cold Storage Fish Market,** downtown on Main Street, or by mail-order (tel. 907/772–4177).

Prince William Sound

Every Gulf of Alaska cruise visits Prince William Sound. The sound made worldwide headlines in 1989, when the *Exxon Valdez* hit a reef and spilled 11 million gallons of North Slope crude. The oil has sunk into the beaches below the surface, however, and vast parts of the sound appear pristine, with abundant wildlife. What lasting effect this lurking oil—which is sometimes uncovered after storms and high tides—will have on the area is still being studied.

Numbers in the margin correspond to points of interest on the South Central Alaska map.

❶ A visit to **Columbia Glacier,** which flows from the surrounding Chugach Mountains, is included on many Gulf of Alaska cruises. Its deep aquamarine face is 5 mi (8 km) across, and it calves new icebergs with resounding cannonades. This glacier is one of the largest and most readily accessible of Alaska's coastal glaciers.

The major attraction in Prince William Sound on most Gulf of Alaska cruises is the day spent in **College Fjord.** **❷** Dubbed "Alaska's newest Glacier Bay" by one cruise line, this deep finger of water is ringed by 16 glaciers, each one named after one of the colleges that sponsored early exploration of the fjord.

72

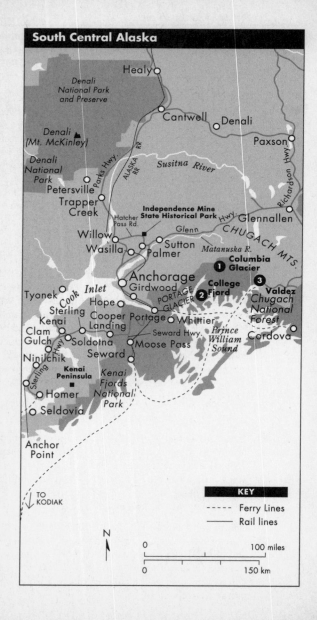

South Central Alaska

Healy

Denali National Park and Preserve

Cantwell

Denali

Paxson

Denali (Mt. McKinley)

Denali National Park

Parks Hwy.

ALASKA RR

RR

Susitna River

Richardson Hwy.

Petersville

Trapper Creek

Hatcher Pass Rd.

Independence Mine State Historical Park

Glenn Hwy.

Glennallen

CHUGACH MTS.

Willow

Wasilla

Palmer

Sutton

Matanuska R.

Columbia Glacier ❶

Anchorage

Girdwood

College Fjord ❷

❸ **Valdez**

Tyonek

Cook Inlet

PORTAGE GLACIER

Chugach National Forest

Sterling

Hope

Portage

Whittier

Cordova

Kenai

Cooper Landing

Prince William Sound

Clam Gulch

Soldotna

Seward Hwy.

Sterling Hwy.

Ninilchik

Moose Pass

Seward

Kenai Peninsula

Kenai Fjords National Park

Homer

Seldovia

Anchor Point

↓ TO KODIAK

N

KEY
- - - Ferry Lines
—— Rail lines

0   100 miles

0   150 km

Of the three major Prince William Sound communities—
❸ Valdez, Whittier, and Cordova—only **Valdez** (pronounced val-*deez*) is a major port of call for cruise ships. For more information on visiting Valdez, *see below.*

Seward

On the southeastern coast of the Kenai Peninsula, Seward is surrounded by four major federal landholdings—**Chugach National Forest, Kenai Wildlife Refuge, Kenai Fjords National Park,** and the **Alaska Maritime National Wildlife Refuge.** The entire area is breathtaking, and you should not miss it in your haste to get to Anchorage.

Seward is one of Alaska's oldest and most scenic communities, set between high mountain ranges on one side and Resurrection Bay on the other. The city was named for U.S. Secretary of State William H. Seward, who was instrumental in arranging the purchase of Alaska from Russia in 1867. Resurrection Bay was named in 1791 by Russian fur trader and explorer Alexander Baranof. The town was established in 1903 by railroad surveyors as an ocean terminal and supply center. The biggest event in Seward's history came after the 1964 Good Friday earthquake—the strongest ever recorded in North America. The tidal wave that followed the quake devastated the town; fortunately, most residents saw the harbor drain almost entirely, knew the wave would follow, and ran to high ground. Since then the town has relied heavily on commercial fishing, and its harbor is important for shipping coal to Asia.

For cruise ship passengers, historic downtown Seward retains its small-town atmosphere; many of its buildings date back to the early 1900s. Modern-day explorers can enjoy wildlife cruise, sportfishing, sailing, and kayaking in the bay, or investigate the intricacies of marine biology at the $52 million **Alaska SeaLife Center,** which opened its doors in 1998.

If you're in Seward on the 4th of July, you'll have the chance to see—and perhaps join—the second oldest footrace in North America. Each year participants race straight up the 3,022-ft trail on Mt. Marathon from downtown. (*See* Hiking, *below.*)

Shore Excursions

Seward is where most passengers taking a Gulf of Alaska cruise get on or off the ship—so most people don't hang around for long. If your ship is one that calls here for the day, or if you're planning to linger a bit longer in town, the following excursions are a good choice. They may not be offered by all cruise lines. All times and prices are approximate.

ADVENTURE

Alaska Railroad Day-Tour. Take a scenic ride on the Alaska Railroad round-trip from Seward to Portage through what the railroad calls "the most scenic part of our route." Food and beverages are sold on board. Trains depart Saturday and Sunday from Seward at noon and return at 5:30 PM. Make reservations in advance by calling 800/544–0552. *Cost: $50.*

IdidaRide Sled-Dog Tours. Seward was the start of the original Iditarod Trail, used to bring medicine to Nome during an epidemic in 1925. Visitors can experience this piece of history by taking a summer sled-dog ride with modern-day Iditarod musher Mitch Seavey. For reservations call 907/224–8607 or 800/478–3139. *1¼ hrs. Cost: $27.50.*

Mt. McKinley Flightseeing. From Anchorage, fly to Denali National Park (filled with bears, wolves, caribou, and moose) to see North America's highest peak. The trip is often canceled due to cloudiness. *3 hrs, 2 hrs flying time. Cost: $288.*

Coming Ashore

Cruise ships dock within ½ mi (1 km) of downtown. The Seward Chamber of Commerce has a visitor information center at the cruise ship dock that is staffed when ships are in port. The Kenai Fjords National Park visitor center (tel. 907/224–3175) is within walking distance: Turn left as you leave the pier, then left again onto 4th Avenue; the center is two blocks ahead. It's open daily, 8 AM to 7 PM. Ask here about visiting scenic Exit Glacier, which is 13 mi (21 km) northwest of Seward. The Alaska National Historical Society operates a book and gift store in the Park Service center. The Chugach National Forest Ranger District office is at 334 4th Avenue.

The **Seward Trolley** (tel. 907/224–8051) stops at the cruise ship dock every half hour and heads to Seward's various points of interest. The cost is $1.50 one-way or $3 round-trip.

Exploring Seward

Seward's newest attraction, is the **Alaska SeaLife Center,** right in town at the south end of 4th Avenue. Funded largely by money from the 1989 Exxon Valdez oil spill settlement, this facility covers a seven-acre site facing Resurrection Bay. Inside, you can watch scientists as they study everything from the genetics of herring to Steller sea lion telemetry. The emphasis is on wildlife research, rehabilitation, and education. No leaping killer whales here, but the centerpieces are the re-created sea and shore habitats—complete with underwater viewing windows—that house seals, sea lions, marine birds, salmon, and other animals. *Tel. 907/ 224–3080. Admission: $12.50. Open daily in summer.*

Although most cruise ship passengers head into Anchorage, there's a great deal to be seen in the Seward area. Don't miss the fjords in Resurrection Bay, with their bird rookeries and sea-lion haulouts. There are numerous tours to choose from—just check out the boardwalk area adjacent to the docks. **Kenai Fjords Tours** (tel. 907/224–8068 or 800/478–8068) has a very good half-day cruise of the bay with a stop for a salmon bake on Fox Island ($59 for a 4-hour dinner cruise, or $74 for a 5-hour lunch cruise). Other tour companies include **Mariah Charters** (tel. 907/243–1238 or 800/ 270–1238), **Kenai Coastal Tours** (tel. 907/224–8068 or 800/770–9119), **Alaska Renown Charters** (tel. 907/224–3806), **Fresh Aire Charters** (tel. 907/272–2755), and **Major Marine Tours** (tel. 907/224–8030 or 800/764–7300).

Thirteen miles (21 kilometers) northeast of Seward, **Exit Glacier** is the only road-accessible part of Kenai Fjords National Park. It's an easy ½ mi (1 km) hike to Exit Glacier from the parking lot; the first ¼ mi (½ km) is paved, which makes it accessible to those using wheelchairs.

If you're looking for history rather than scenery and wildlife, check out the **Seward Museum,** which has exhibits on the 1964 earthquake, the Iditarod, and Native history. *Corner* *of 3rd and Jefferson, tel. 907/224–3902. Admission: $2. Open daily 9–5.*

Across from the museum is the **1916 Rail Car Seward.** Once part of the Alaska's Railroad's rolling stock, it today is permanently parked here as an information center. Displays inside detail the 1964 Good Friday earthquake and how it devastated the town of Seward.

Shopping

Local gift and souvenir shops include the **Alaska Shop** (210 4th Ave., tel. 907/224–5420), **Bardarson Studio** (Small Boat Harbor, tel. 907/224–5448), and the **Treasure Chest** (Small Boat Harbor, tel. 907/224–8087). One of the best options is **Resurrect Art Coffeehouse Gallery** (320 3rd Ave., tel. 907/224–7161; *see* Dining, *below*), where you'll find jewelry, pottery, books, prints, and paintings by local artisans.

Ranting Raven Bakery (228 4th Ave., tel. 907/224–2228) has a gift shop stocked with Russian and Ukrainian imports. Don't forget to try the home-baked breads, pastries, and cakes.

Sports

FISHING

Every August the **Seward Silver Salmon Derby** attracts hundreds of folks who compete for the $10,000 top prize. For fishing, sightseeing, and drop-off/pickup tours, contact **Fish House** (tel. 907/224–3674 or 800/257–7760), Seward's oldest operator.

HIKING

The strenuous **Mt. Marathon** trail starts at the west end of Lowell Canyon Road and runs practically straight uphill. An easier and more convenient hike for cruise passengers is the **Two Lakes Trail,** a loop of footpaths and bridges on the edge of town. A map is available from the Seward Chamber of Commerce (tel. 907/224–8051).

Dining

$$ **Ray's Waterfront.** When it comes to seafood, Ray's is the place. The walls are lined with trophy fish, and the windows front the busy harbor. It's a favorite place to grab a bite to eat while waiting for your tour boat, or to relax with a cocktail as the sun goes down. The menu includes deli-

cious mesquite-grilled salmon, plus clam chowder, crab, and other fresh-from-the-sea specialties. *On the Small Boat Harbor, tel. 907/224–5632. AE, DC, MC, V.*

$–$$ **Harbor Dinner Club & Lounge.** Stop at this spot in Seward's historic downtown district for solid lunch fare including burgers, sandwiches, and clam chowder. The outside deck is a good place to dine on a sunny summer afternoon. You'll find prime rib, steaks, and seafood on the dinner menu. *220 5th Ave., tel. 907/224–3012. AE, D, DC, MC, V.*

$ **Resurrect Art Coffeehouse Gallery.** Built in 1916–17, it served for many years as a Lutheran church. Today, locals and tourists come to worship the espresso coffee and pastries on rainy days, or for live music and poetry on summer evenings. *320 3rd Ave., tel. 907/224–7161. No credit cards.*

Sitka

For hundreds of years before the 18th-century arrival of the Russians, Sitka was home to the Tlingit people. But Sitka's protected harbor, mild climate, and economic potential caught the attention of outsiders. Russian Territorial Governor Alexander Baranof saw in the island's massive timbered forests raw materials for shipbuilding, and its location suited trading routes to California, Hawaii, and the Orient. In 1799 Baranof established an outpost that he called Redoubt St. Michael, 6 mi (10 km) north of the present town, and moved a large number of his Russian and Aleut fur hunters there from Kodiak Island.

The Tlingits attacked Baranof's people and burned his buildings in 1802, but Baranof returned in 1804 with a formidable force, including shipboard cannons. He attacked the Tlingits at their fort near Indian River (site of the present-day, 105-acre Sitka National Historical Park) and drove them to the other side of the island. The Tlingits and Russians made peace in 1821, and, eventually, the capital of Russian America was shifted to Sitka from Kodiak.

Sitka today is known primarily for its onion-dome Russian Orthodox church, one of Southeast Alaska's most famous landmarks, and the Alaska Raptor Rehabilitation Center, a hospital for injured bald eagles and other birds of prey. But don't miss the 15 totem poles scattered throughout the grounds of the national historical park.

Shore Excursions

The following is a good choice in Sitka. It may not be offered by all cruise lines. All times and prices are approximate.

ADVENTURE

Kayak Adventure. Get down to sea level to search for marine and land wildlife in two-person sea kayaks. Sightings of eagles, seals, bears, and deer are likely. If your ship doesn't offer this excursion, contact Baidarka Boats (*see* Sea Kayaking, *below*). *3 hrs, includes 1½ hrs of kayaking. Cost: $78.*

DANCE

The 40 members (all women) of the **New Archangel Dancers** perform Russian dances at Centennial Hall when cruise ships are in port. Call 907/747–5940 for details.

Coming Ashore

Only the smallest excursion vessels can dock at Sitka. Ocean liners must drop anchor in the harbor and tender passengers ashore near Centennial Hall, with its big Tlingit war canoe. Inside is the Sitka Visitors Bureau information desk, which provides maps and brochures.

Sitka is hilly, but the waterfront attractions are an easy walk from the tender landing. You may, however, want to consider a taxi if you're heading all the way to the other side of the harbor.

Exploring Sitka

Numbers in the margin correspond to points of interest on the Sitka map.

To get one of the best views in town, turn left on Harbor Drive and head for **Castle Hill,** where Alaska was handed over to the United States on October 18, 1867, and where the first 49-star U.S. flag was flown on January 3, 1959, signifying the spirit of Alaska's statehood. Take the first right off Harbor Drive, then look for the entrance to Baranof Castle Hill State Historic Site. Make a left on the gravel path that takes you to the top of the hill overlooking Crescent Harbor.

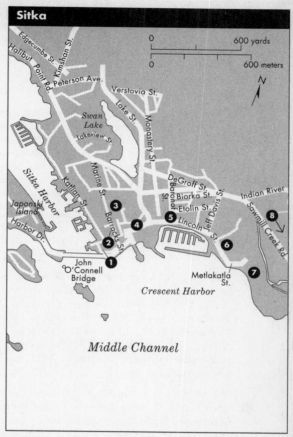

Sitka

Alaska Raptor
Rehabilitation
Center, 8
Castle Hill, 1
Russian
Bishop's
House, 5
Russian and
Lutheran
Cemetery, 3

St. Michael's
Cathedral, 4
Sheldon
Jackson
Museum, 6
Sitka National
Historical
Park Visitor
Center, 7

Sitka State
Pioneers'
Home, 2

❷ The **Sitka State Pioneers' Home** was built in 1934 as the first of several state-run retirement homes and medical-care facilities. The statue, symbolizing the state's sourdoughs (as old-timers are nicknamed), was modeled after an authentic pioneer, William "Skagway Bill" Fonda. It portrays a determined prospector with pack, pick, rifle, and supplies, headed for gold country.

Three old anchors, believed to be from 19th-century British ships, mark **Totem Square.** Notice the double-headed eagle of czarist Russia on the park's totem pole. Just up the street from the Pioneers' Home is the **Shee'ka Kwaan Naa Kahidi Performing Arts Center,** with demonstrations and performances by members of the Sitka tribe. A small museum here houses historic prints and displays on edible plants.

❸ The most distinctive grave in the **Russian and Lutheran cemetery** marks the final resting place of Princess Maksoutoff, one of the most famous members of the Russian royal family buried on Alaskan soil.

❹ Sitka's most photographed sight, **St. Michael's Cathedral** had its origins in a frame-covered log structure built in the 1840s. In 1966 the church burned in a fire that swept through the business district. Using original blueprints, an almost-exact replica of St. Michael's was built and dedicated in 1976. *Lincoln St., tel. 907/747–8120. Admission: $1 donation requested. Open daily 7:30 AM–5:30 PM and when cruise ships are in port.*

❺ Several blocks past St. Michael's Cathedral on Lincoln Street and facing the harbor is the **Russian Bishop's House.** Constructed in 1842, this is one of the few remaining Russian log homes in Alaska. The Park Service has carefully restored the building, using original Russian furnishings and artifacts. In one room a portion of the house's structure has been peeled away to expose 19th-century building techniques. *Lincoln St., tel. 907/747–6281. Donation requested. Open daily 9–1 and 2–5.*

❻ The octagonal **Sheldon Jackson Museum,** built in 1895, contains priceless Native American items collected by Dr. Sheldon Jackson from the remote regions of Alaska. Carved masks, Chilkat blankets, dogsleds, kayaks—even the helmet worn by Chief Katlean during the 1804 battle between the

Sitka Tlingits and the Russians—are displayed here. *Lincoln St., tel. 907/747–8981. Admission: $3. Open daily 8–5.*

7 **Sitka National Historical Park Visitor Center** is at the far end of Lincoln Street. Audiovisual programs and exhibits, including native and Russian artifacts, give an overview of Southeast Alaskan cultures, both old and new. Native artists and craftspeople are on hand to demonstrate and interpret traditional crafts of the Tlingit people, such as silversmithing, weaving, and basketry. A self-guided trail (maps available at the visitor center) to the site of the Tlingit Fort passes by some of the most skillfully carved totem poles in the state; some of these 15 poles date back more than nine decades. *Tel. 907/747–6281. Admission free. Open daily 8–5.*

8 One of Sitka's most interesting attractions is the **Alaska Raptor Rehabilitation Center,** where injured birds of prey are nursed back to health. A visit to this unusual nature center rarely disappoints. *1101 Sawmill Creek Rd., tel. 907/747–8662. Admission: $10. Open daily 8–5, and when cruise ship passengers are in port.*

Shopping
Several local shops sell quality crafts and gifts, including **Sitka Rose Gallery** (419 Lincoln St., tel. 907/747–3030) and the **Sitka Crafters Mall** (110 American St., tel. 907/747–6544). Native jewelry and other handicrafts are available from the **Sitka National Historical Park Visitor Center** (*see* Exploring Sitka, *above*).

A few stores, such as the **Russian-American Company** (407 Lincoln St., tel. 907/747–6228) and the **New Archangel Trading Co.** (335 Harbor Dr., across from Centennial Hall, tel. 907/747–8181), sell Russian items, including the popular *matruchka* nesting dolls.

For books on Alaska, stop by **Old Harbor Books** (201 Lincoln St., tel. 907/747–8808).

Sports
FISHING
Fishing is excellent here. Contact **Steller Charters** (tel. 907/747–6167) or see the information desk in Centennial Hall for a list of other charter operators.

Sitka's easiest hiking can be done along the 2 mi (3 km) of trails in **Sitka National Historical Park.** Here you can find some of the most dramatically situated totem poles in Alaska, relax at the picnic areas, and watch spawning salmon during the seasonal runs on the Indian River.

Several local companies offer guided sea-kayak trips, but you won't go wrong with **Baidarka Boats** (above Old Harbor Books at 201 Lincoln St., tel. 907/747-8996). Half-day trips are $50 for a double kayak. Be sure to make arrangements in advance so that your guide and/or kayak is waiting for you at the harbor.

Dining

$ **Backdoor Cafe.** For a dose of Sitka's caffeine-fueled hip side, scoot on through Old Harbor Books to this cozy latte joint. Good pastries and bagels too. *201 Lincoln St., tel. 907/747–8856. No credit cards.*

$ **Bay View Restaurant.** Conveniently located for passengers touring the historic waterfront, the Bay View has Russian specialties that reflect Sitka's colonial heritage. Gourmet burgers (including one with caviar) and deli sandwiches are also available, as is beer and wine. *407 Lincoln St., tel. 907/747–5440. AE, MC, V.*

Saloons

Pilot House (713 Katlean St., tel. 907/747–4707) is a dance spot with a waterfront view.

Pioneer Bar (212 Katlean St., tel. 907/747–3456), across from the harbor, is a hangout for local fishermen. Tourists get a kick out of its authentic Alaskan ambience; the walls are lined with pictures of local fishing boats.

Skagway

The early gold-rush days of Alaska, when dreamers and hooligans descended on the Yukon via the murderous White Pass, are preserved in Skagway. Now a part of the Klondike Gold Rush National Historical Park, downtown Skagway was once the picturesque but sometimes lawless gateway for the frenzied stampede to the interior goldfields.

Local park rangers and residents now interpret and re-create that remarkable era for visitors. Old false-front stores, saloons, brothels, and wood sidewalks have been completely restored. You'll be regaled with tall tales of con artists, golden-hearted "ladies," stampeders, and newsmen. Such colorful characters as outlaw Jefferson "Soapy" Smith and his gang earned the town a reputation so bad that, by the spring of 1898, the superintendent of the Northwest Royal Mounted Police had labeled Skagway "little better than a hell on earth." But Soapy was killed in a duel with surveyor Frank Reid, and soon a civilizing influence, in the form of churches and family life, prevailed. When the gold played out just a few years later, the town of 20,000 dwindled to its current population of just over 700 (twice that in the summer months).

Shore Excursions

The following are good choices in Skagway. They may not be offered by all cruise lines. All times and prices are approximate.

ADVENTURE

Bike the Klondike. By van, travel to the top of the 3,000-ft Klondike Pass. Then by mountain bike, coast 15 mi (24 km) down a moderate grade, enjoying the spectacular views of the White Pass along the way. Great photo opportunities, including the waterfalls, glaciers, and coastal mountains, abound. All equipment is included. *2 hrs. Cost: $70.*

Glacier Bay Flightseeing. If your ship doesn't sail through Glacier Bay—or even if it does—here's your chance to see it from above. *2 hrs, including 90-min flight. Cost: $110–$135.*

Gold Rush Helicopter Tour. Fly over the Chilkoot Gold Rush Trail into a remote mountain valley for a landing on a glacier. Special boots are provided for walking on the glacier. *2 hrs, including 50-min flight. Cost: $150–$220.*

GOLD RUSH HISTORY

White Pass and Yukon Railroad. The 20-mi (32-km) trip in vintage railroad cars, on narrow-gauge tracks built to serve the Yukon goldfields, runs past the infamous White Pass, skims along the edge of granite cliffs, crosses a 215-ft-high steel cantilever bridge over Dead Horse Gulch, climbs to a 2,865-ft elevation at White Pass Summit, and zigzags through dramatic scenery—including the actual Trail of '98, worn into the mountainside a century ago. A must for railroad buffs; great for children. *3 hrs. Cost: $80–$90.*

Coming Ashore

Cruise ships dock just a short stroll from downtown Skagway. From the pier you can see the large yellow-and-red White Pass & Yukon Railroad Depot, now the National Park Service Visitor Center. Inside is an excellent photographic exhibit and a superb documentary film. Ask the rangers about nearby hiking trails and exploring the gold rush cemetery. Information on local history and attractions is also available from the **Skagway Visitor Information Center** (333 5th Ave., ½ block off Broadway, tel. 907/ 983–2855).

Virtually all the shops and gold rush sights are along Broadway, the main strip that leads from the visitor center through the middle of town, so you really don't need a taxi. Horse-drawn surreys, antique limousines, and modern vans pick up passengers at the pier and along Broadway for tours. The tracks of the White Pass and Yukon Railway run right along the pier; train departures are coordinated with cruise ship arrivals.

Exploring Skagway

Numbers in the margin correspond to points of interest on the Skagway map.

Skagway is perhaps the easiest port in Alaska to explore on foot. Just walk up and down Broadway, detouring here and there into the side streets. Keep an eye out for the humorous architectural details and advertising irreverence that mark the Skagway spirit.

❶ From the cruise ship dock, follow the road into town to the **Red Onion Saloon,** where a lady-of-the-evening mannequin peers down from the former second-floor brothel, and drinks are still served on the original mahogany bar. *Broadway and 2nd Ave., tel. 907/983–2222.*

❷ You can't help but notice the **Arctic Brotherhood Hall/Trail of '98 Museum,** with its curious driftwood-mosaic facade.

In case you want to see the world.

At American Express, we're here to make your journey a smooth one. So we have over 1,700 travel service locations in over 120 countries ready to help. What else would you expect from the world's largest travel agency?

do more ®

Travel

http://www.americanexpress.com/travel

In case you want to be welcomed there.

We're here to see that you're always welcomed at establishments everywhere. That's why millions of people carry the American Express® Card — for peace of mind, confidence, and security, around the world or just around the corner.

do more®

In case you're running low.

We're here to help with more than **118,000 Express Cash** locations around the world. In order to enroll, just call American Express before you start your vacation.

do more

Express Cash

And just in case.

We're here with American Express® Travelers Cheques
and Cheques *for Two.®* They're the safest way to carry
money on your vacation and the surest way to get a
refund, practically anywhere, anytime.
Another way we help you...

do more

AMERICAN
EXPRESS

Travelers
Cheques

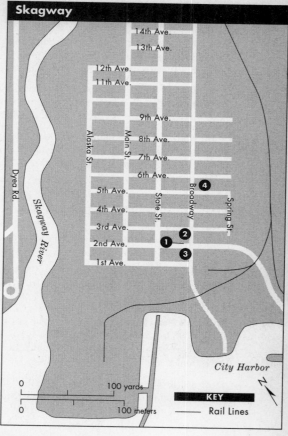

Skagway

14th Ave.
13th Ave.
12th Ave.
11th Ave.
9th Ave.
8th Ave.
7th Ave.
6th Ave.
5th Ave.
4th Ave.
3rd Ave.
2nd Ave.
1st Ave.

Alaska St.
Main St.
State St.
Broadway
Spring St.
Dyea Rd.
Skagway River

City Harbor

0 — 100 yards
0 — 100 meters

KEY
— Rail Lines

Arctic Brotherhood Hall/Trail of '98 Museum, **2**
Eagles Hall, **4**

Red Onion Saloon, **1**
Soapy's Parlor, **3**

Broadway between 2nd Ave. and 3rd Ave., tel. 907/983–2420. Open when cruise ships are in port.

A small, almost inconsequential shack on 2nd Avenue was **❸ Soapy's Parlor**—named after the notorious, gold-rush con man—but it's not open to tourists. *Off Broadway.*

You'll find down-home sourdough cooking at the **Golden North Hotel.** Founded in 1898, it bills itself as the oldest hotel in Alaska. *Broadway and 3rd Ave., tel. 907/983–2451.*

A rip-roaring revue, "Skagway in the Days of '98," is **❹** staged at the **Eagles Hall.** *Broadway and 6th Ave., tel. 907/983–2545. Admission: $15. Performances scheduled when cruise ships are in port.*

Shopping
Broadway is filled with numerous curio shops selling unusual merchandise. Although prices tend to be high as a general rule, good deals can be found, so shop around and don't buy the first thing you see.

David Present's Gallery (Broadway and 3rd Ave., tel. 907/983–2873) has outstanding but pricey art by Alaskan artists.

Dedman's Photo Shop (Broadway between 3rd and 4th Aves., tel. 907/983–2353) has been a Skagway institution since the early days; here you'll find unusual historical photos, guidebooks, and old-fashioned newspapers.

Kirmse's (Broadway and 5th Ave., tel. 907/983–2822) has a large selection of expensive, inexpensive, and downright tacky souvenirs. On display is the world's largest, heaviest, and most valuable gold-nugget watch chain.

Sports
HIKING
Real wilderness is within a stone's throw of the docks, which makes this an excellent hiking port. Try the short jaunt to beautiful **Lower Dewey Lake.** Start at the corner of 4th Avenue and Spring Street, go toward the mountain, cross the footbridge over Pullen Creek, and follow the trail uphill.

A less strenuous hike is the trip through **Gold Rush Cemetery,** where the epitaphs offer strange but lively bits of social commentary. To get there, keep walking up Broadway, turn left onto 8th Avenue, then right onto State Street. Go through the railroad yards and follow the signs to the cemetery, which is 1½ mi (3 km), or a 30- to 45-minute walk, from town. To reach 300-ft-high **Reid Falls,** continue through the cemetery for ¼ mi (½ km). The National Park Service Visitor Center offers trail maps, advice, and the helpful brochure, *Skagway Gold Rush Cemetery Guide.* Trail maps also are available at the **City Visitor Center** (333 5th Ave., ½ block off Broadway, tel. 907/983–2855).

Dining

$$$ **Lorna's at the Skagway Inn.** This is Skagway's upmarket restaurant, with a French-trained chef who specializes in artfully prepared Alaskan seafood. Guaranteed to please your palate, though your wallet will be a bit worse for the experience. Lorna's also has a great wine and dessert selection. *7th Ave. and Broadway, tel. 907/983–3161. MC, V.*

$–$$ **Golden North Restaurant.** To eat in the Golden North Hotel's dining room is to return to the days of gold-rush con man Soapy Smith, heroic Frank Reid, and scores of pioneers, stampeders, and dance-hall girls. The decor is authentic and has been tastefully restored. Try the sourdough pancakes for breakfast. *3rd Ave. and Broadway, tel. 907/ 983–2294. AE, DC, MC, V.*

Saloons

Moe's Frontier Bar (Broadway between 4th and 5th streets, tel. 907/983–2238). A longtime fixture on the Skagway scene, Moe's is a bar much frequented by the local folk.

Red Onion (Broadway at 2nd St., tel. 907/983–2222). You'll meet at least as many Skagway people here as you will visitors. There's live music on Thursday nights, ranging from rock and jazz to folk and acoustic. The upstairs was a gold-rush brothel.

Tracy Arm

Like Misty Fjords (*see above*), Tracy Arm and its sister fjord, Endicott Arm, have become staples on many Inside Passage cruises. Ships sail into the arm just before or after a visit to Juneau, the state capital, 50 mi (80 km) to the north. A day of scenic cruising in Tracy Arm is a lesson in geology and the forces that shaped Alaska. The fjord was carved by a glacier eons ago, leaving behind sheer granite cliffs. Waterfalls continue the process of erosion that the glaciers began. Very small ships may nudge their bows under the waterfalls, so crew members can fill pitchers full of glacial runoff. It's a uniquely Alaskan refreshment. Tracy Arm's glaciers haven't disappeared, though, they've just receded, and at the very end of Tracy Arm you'll come to two of them, known collectively as the twin Sawyer Glaciers.

Valdez

Valdez, with its year-round ice-free port, was an entry point for people and goods going to the interior during the gold rush. Today that flow has been reversed, and Valdez Harbor is the southern terminus of the Trans-Alaska pipeline, which carries crude oil from Prudhoe Bay and surrounding oil fields nearly 800 mi (1,287 km) to the north.

Much of Valdez looks new because the business area was relocated and rebuilt after being destroyed by the devastating Good Friday earthquake in 1964. A few of the old buildings were moved to the new town site.

Many Alaskan communities have summer fishing derbies, but Valdez may hold the record for the number of such contests, stretching from late May into September for halibut and various runs of salmon. The Valdez Silver Salmon Derby begins in late July and runs the entire month of August. Fishing charters abound in this area of Prince William Sound, and for a good reason, too: These fertile waters provide some of the best saltwater sportfishing in all of Alaska.

Shore Excursions

The following are good choices in Valdez. They may not be offered by all cruise lines. All times and prices are approximate.

ADVENTURE

Columbia Glacier Floatplane Sightseeing. Enjoy aerial views of Valdez and Shoup Glacier, a section of the pipeline, and its terminus. The highlight is touching down in the water for a close-up view of the massive Columbia Glacier. 1½

*hrs, including 1-hr flight and 15-min landing on glacier.
Cost: $179.*

Columbia Glacier Helicopter Flightseeing. The flight over
the huge Columbia Glacier includes a landing near the face
of Shoup Glacier and aerial views of Valdez Bay, the pipeline
terminus, and the old Valdez site. *1¼ hrs, including 45-min
flight. Cost: $150–$200.*

Keystone River Rafting. This 1½-hour raft trip goes down
the Lowe River, through a scenic canyon, and past the
spectacular Bridal Veil Falls, which cascades 900 ft down
the canyon wall. The bus trip from the ship is narrated. *2¼
hrs. Cost: $60–$70.*

Sea-kayaking Adventures. Get down on the water's surface
for a guided tour of the port of Valdez or Robe Lake. See a
seabird rookery and seals up close or float across the mir-
rorlike surface of a freshwater lake tucked against the bot-
tom of the Chugach Mountains. *4–6 hrs. Cost: $52–$185.*

TRANS-ALASKA PIPELINE

Pipeline Story. Tour the pipeline terminus and hear tales of
how the pipeline was built. This is the only way to get into
this high-security area. *2¼ hrs. Cost: $24.*

Coming Ashore

Ships tie up at the world's largest floating container dock.
About 3 mi (5 km) from the heart of town, the dock is used
not only for cruise ships, but also for loading cargo ships
with timber and other products bound for markets "outside" (that's what Alaskans call the rest of the world).

Ship-organized motor coaches meet passengers on the pier
and provide transportation into town. Cabs and car-rental
services will also provide transportation from the pier. Several local ground and adventure-tour operators meet passengers as well.

Once in town, you'll find that Valdez is a very compact community. Almost everything is within easy walking distance
of the Valdez Convention and Visitors Bureau in the heart
of town. Motor coaches drop passengers at the Visitor Information Center. Taxi service is available and individual-
ized tours of the area can be arranged with the cab dispatcher.

Exploring Valdez

Other than visiting the oil-pipeline terminal, which must be done on a tour, sightseeing in Valdez is mostly limited to gazing at the 5,000-ft mountain peaks surrounding the town or visiting the **Valdez Museum.** It depicts the lives, livelihoods, and events significant to Valdez and surrounding regions. Exhibits include a 1907 steam fire engine, a 19th-century saloon, and a model of the pipeline terminus. *217 Egan Ave., tel. 907/835–2764. Admission: $3. Open daily 8–8.*

Dining

$–$$ Mike's Palace. This busy restaurant with typical Italian-diner decor serves great pizzas, lasagna, beer-batter halibut, and Greek specialties, including gyros. *On the harbor, 201 N. Harbor Dr., tel. 907/835–2365. MC, V.*

Vancouver, British Columbia

Cosmopolitan Vancouver, Canada's answer to San Francisco, enjoys a spectacular setting. Tall fir trees stand practically downtown, rock spires tower close by, the ocean laps at your doorstep, and people from every corner of the earth create a youthful and vibrant atmosphere.

Vancouver is a young city, even by North American standards. It was not yet a town in 1870, when British Columbia became part of the Canadian confederation. The city's history, such as it is, remains visible to the naked eye: Eras are stacked east to west along the waterfront like some century-old archaeological dig—from cobblestoned, late-Victorian Gastown to shiny postmodern glass cathedrals of commerce grazing the sunset.

Shore Excursions

Unless you're on a longer cruise that begins in Los Angeles or San Francisco, Vancouver will likely be your first or last stop. If you're sailing round-trip, you'll get on and off the ship in Vancouver (*see* Chapter 4). Because most passengers are busy transferring between the airport and the ship, few shore excursions are scheduled. If you plan to stay in Vancouver before or after your cruise, most lines sell pre- or post-cruise city packages.

For cruise passengers on longer cruises, a call in Vancouver will be much like any other port call: You'll disembark just for the day and have the option of taking a ship organized tour or exploring independently.

The following are good choices in Vancouver. They may not be offered by all cruise lines. Times and prices are approximate.

City Tour. If this is your first visit to Vancouver, a city tour is a convenient way to see all the sights of this cosmopolitan city—the largest you'll visit on an Alaska cruise. Highlights include the Gastown district, Chinatown, and Stanley Park. *3 hrs. Cost: $29.*

Vancouver Pre- or Post-Cruise Package. Cruise-line land packages are an easy way to extend your cruise vacation without making separate arrangements. Usually, you'll have a choice of one, two, or three nights in town. Often, you'll also have a choice of hotels (in different price ranges). Most packages include sightseeing tours and transfers between the ship and the hotel. Meals are generally extra unless noted in the brochure; transfers between the airport and hotel may be included only for air-sea passengers. Check with your cruise line or travel agent for the exact terms of your Vancouver package.

Coming Ashore

Most ships dock downtown at the Canada Place cruise-ship terminal—instantly recognizable by its rooftop of dramatic white sails. A few vessels tie up at the nearby Ballantyne cruise terminal. Both are within minutes of the city center. Stop off at Tourism Vancouver Infocentre across the street (next door to the Waterfront Centre Hotel) to pick up brochures on other Vancouver attractions and events before leaving the pier area.

Many sights of interest are concentrated in the hemmed-in peninsula of Downtown Vancouver. The heart of Vancouver—which includes the downtown area, Stanley Park, and the West End high-rise residential neighborhood—sits on this peninsula bordered by English Bay and the Pacific Ocean to the west; by False Creek, the inlet home to Granville Island, to the south; and by Burrard Inlet, the working port of the city, to the north, past which loom the

North Shore mountains. The oldest part of the city—Gastown and Chinatown—lies at the edge of Burrard Inlet, around Main Street, which runs north–south and is roughly the dividing line between the east side and the west side. All the avenues, which are numbered, have east and west designations.

It is difficult to hail a cab in Vancouver; unless you're near a hotel, you'd have better luck calling a taxi service. Try **Yellow** (tel. 604/681–3311) or **Black Top** (tel. 604/681–2181).

Exploring Vancouver

Numbers in the margin correspond to points of interest on the Downtown Vancouver map. Prices are given in Canadian dollars.

❶ At **Canada Place,** walk along the promenade on the pier's west side for fine views of the Burrard Inlet harbor and Stanley Park.

❷ The **Canadian Craft Museum,** which opened in 1992, is one of the first national cultural facilities dedicated to crafts—historical and contemporary, functional and decorative. Examples here range from elegantly carved utensils with decorative handles to colorful hand-spun and handwoven garments. *639 Hornby St., tel. 604/687–8266. Admission: $4. Open Mon.–Sat. 10–5, Sun. and holidays noon–5.*

❸ **Gastown** is where Vancouver originated after Jack Deighton arrived at Burrard Inlet in 1867 with his Indian wife, a barrel of whiskey, and few amenities and set up a saloon to entertain the scattered loggers and trappers living in the area. When the transcontinental train arrived in 1887, Gastown became the transfer point for trade with the Orient and was soon crowded with hotels and warehouses. The Klondike gold rush encouraged further development until 1912, when the "Golden Years" ended. From the 1930s to the 1950s hotels were converted into rooming houses, and the warehouse district shifted elsewhere. The neglected area gradually became run-down. However, both Gastown and Chinatown were declared historic districts in the late 1970s and have been revitalized. Gastown is now chockablock with boutiques, cafés, and souvenir shops.

The Chinese were among the first inhabitants of Vancouver, and some of the oldest buildings in the city are in **Chinatown.** There was already a sizable Chinese community in British Columbia because of the 1858 Cariboo gold rush in central British Columbia, but the greatest influx from China came in the 1880s, during construction of the Canadian Pacific Railway, when 15,000 laborers were imported. It is best to view the buildings in Chinatown from the south side of Pender Street, where the Chinese Cultural Center stands. From here you'll see important details that adorn the upper stories. The style of architecture in Vancouver's Chinatown is patterned on that of Canton and won't be seen in any other Canadian cities.

Stanley Park is a 1,000-acre wilderness park just blocks from the downtown section of the city. An afternoon in Stanley Park gives you a capsule tour of Vancouver that includes beaches, the ocean, the harbor, Douglas fir and cedar forests, and a good look at the North Shore mountains. The park sits on a peninsula, and along the shore is a pathway 9 km (5½ mi) long, called the seawall. You can drive or bicycle all the way around. Bicycles are for rent at the foot of Georgia Street near the park entrance. Cyclists must ride in a counterclockwise direction and stay on their side of the path.

The totem poles you'll see in Stanley Park were not made in the Vancouver area; these, carved of cedar by the Kwakiutl and Haida peoples late in the last century, were brought to the park from the north coast of British Columbia. There's also an aquarium (tel. 604/682–1118) within the park grounds, where you can see the sealife of coastal British Columbia, the Canadian arctic, and other areas of the world.

Shopping
Unlike many cities where suburban malls have taken over, Vancouver has a downtown that is still lined with individual boutiques and specialty shops. Stores are usually open daily and on Thursday and Friday nights, and Sunday noon to 5.

Robson Street, stretching from Burrard to Bute streets, is chockablock with small boutiques and cafés. Vancouver's

94

TO
STANLEY
PARK

Broughton

Cana

Hastings

Pender

Tourism
Vancouver

Jervis

Melville

Hastings

Georgia

Bute

Alberni

Burrard

Robson

Hornby

Haro

Thurlow

Howe

Pender

Barclay

Dunsmuir

Nelson

Georgia

Comox

Granville St.

Robson

Seymour

Burrard

Richards

Hornby

Smithe

Homer

Howe

Canada Place, **1**
Canadian Craft
Museum, **2**
Chinatown, **4**
Gastown, **3**

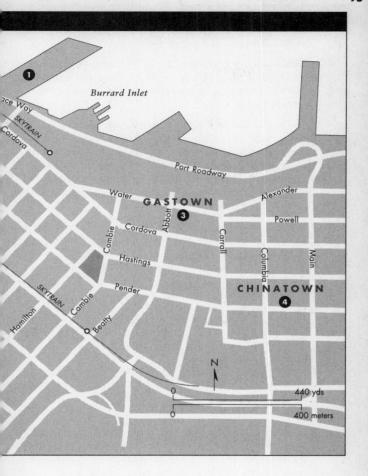

Burrard Inlet

❶

ce Way

SKYTRAIN

Cordova

Port Roadway

Water

GASTOWN

❸

Alexander

Powell

Cordova

Abbott

Cambie

Carrall

Hastings

Columbia

Main

CHINATOWN

❹

Pender

SKYTRAIN

Cambie

Hamilton

Beatty

N

0

440 yds

0

400 meters

liveliest street is not only for the fashion-conscious; it also provides many excellent corners for people-watching and attracts an array of street performers.

Chinatown (*see* Exploring Vancouver, *above*)—centered on Pender and Main streets—is an exciting and animated place for restaurants, exotic foods, and distinctive architecture.

For books, **Duthie's** (919 Robson St., tel. 604/684–4496) downtown is a favorite in Vancouver. Fashion is big business in Vancouver, and there are clothing boutiques on almost every corner downtown. If your tastes are traditional, don't miss **George Straith** (900 W. Georgia St., tel. 604/685–3301) in the Hotel Vancouver, offering tailored designer fashions for both sexes.

Want something special to take home from British Columbia? One of the best places in Vancouver for good-quality souvenirs (West Coast native art, books, music, jewelry, and so on) is the **Clamshell Gift Shop** (Vancouver Aquarium, tel. 604/685–5911) in Stanley Park. In Gastown, Haida, Inuit, and Salish, native art is available at **Images for a Canadian Heritage** (164 Water St., tel. 604/685–7046), as is a selection of fine Canadian crafts.

Sports
BIKING

Stanley Park (*see* Stanley Park, *above*) is the most popular spot for family cycling. Rentals are available here from Bayshore Bicycles (745 Denman St., tel. 604/688–2453) or Stanley Park Rentals (1798 W. Georgia, tel. 604/681–5581).

GOLF

One of the finest public courses in the country is **Peace Portal** (6900 4th Ave., tel. 604/538–4818), near White Rock, a 45-minute drive from downtown.

Dining
$$ **Five Sails.** On the fourth floor of the Pan Pacific Hotel, this special-occasion restaurant affords a stunning panoramic view of Canada Place, Lions Gate Bridge, and the lights of the north shore across the bay. Austrian chef Ernst Dorfler has a special flair for presentation, from the swan-shape butter served with breads early in the meal to the choco-

late ice-cream bonbon served at the end. The broad-reaching, seasonally changing Pacific Rim menu often includes caramelized swordfish, spicy Mongolian-style chicken, and such old favorites as medallions of British Columbia salmon or lamb from Salt Spring Island. *Pan Pacific Hotel, 300–999 Canada Pl., tel. 604/662–8211. Reservations essential. AE, DC, MC, V. No lunch.*

$$ Imperial Chinese Seafood. This elegant Cantonese restaurant in the art deco Marine Building offers stupendous views through two-story floor-to-ceiling windows of Stanley Park and the North Shore mountains across Coal Harbour. Any dish featuring lobster, crab, or shrimp from the live tanks is recommended, as is the dim sum served every day from 11 to 2:30. Portions tend to be small and pricey (especially the abalone, shark's fin, and bird's-nest delicacies) but never fail to please. *355 Burrard St., tel. 604/688–8191. Reservations essential. AE, MC, V.*

$$ Joe Fortes Seafood House. Reserve a table on the second floor balcony at this Vancouver seafood hot spot to take in the view of the broad wall murals and the mounted blue marlins. The signature panfried Cajun oysters, clam and corn fritters, salmon with smoked apple and cider chutney, and seared sea scallops in sesame and oyster glaze are tasty and filling, but often overlooked in favor of the reasonably priced daily special. *777 Thurlow St., tel. 604/669–1940. Reservations essential. AE, D, DC, MC, V.*

$ Olympia Fish Market and Oyster Co. Ltd. Owner Carlo Sorace fries up some of the city's best fish-and-chips in this tiny shop behind a fish store in the middle of the Robson Street shopping district. The choice is halibut, cod, prawns, calamari, and whatever's on special in the store, served with homemade coleslaw and genuine—never frozen—french fries. It's funky and fun. *1094 Robson St., tel. 604/685–0716. Reservations not accepted. DC, MC, V.*

Bars and Lounges

The **Gérard Lounge** (845 Burrard St., tel. 604/682–5511) at the Sutton Place Hotel, with its Old World ambience, is probably the nicest in the city. For spectacular views, head up to the **Roof Lounge** (900 W. Georgia St., tel. 604/684–3131) in the Hotel Vancouver, where a band plays contemporary dance music nightly. The **Bacchus Lounge** (845 Hornby St., tel. 604/689–7777) in the Wedgewood Hotel is stylish and sophisticated. The **Garden Terrace** (791 W. Georgia St., tel. 604/689–9333) in the Four Seasons is bright and airy with greenery and a waterfall, plus big soft chairs you won't want to get out of; a pianist plays here on the weekends.

Microbreweries have finally hit Vancouver. At **Steam Works** (375 Water St., tel. 604/689–2739) on the edge of bustling Gastown, they use an age-old steam brewing process and large copper kettles (visible through glass walls in the dining room downstairs) to whip up six to nine brews; the espresso ale is interesting. The **Yaletown Brewing Company** (1111 Mainland St., tel. 604/681–2739) is based in a huge renovated warehouse with a glassed-in brewery turning out eight tasty microbrews; it also has a darts and billiards pub and a restaurant with an open-grill kitchen.

Victoria, British Columbia

Though Victoria is not in Alaska, it is a port of call for many ships cruising the Inside Passage. Just like the communities of Southeast Alaska, Victoria had its own gold rush stampede in the 1800s, when 25,000 miners flocked to British Columbia's Cariboo country. Today the city is a mix of stately buildings and English traditions. Flower baskets hang from lampposts, shops sell Harris tweed and Irish linen, locals play cricket and croquet, and visitors sightsee aboard red double-decker buses or horse-drawn carriages. Afternoon tea is still held daily at the city's elegant Empress Hotel. No visit to Victoria is complete without a stroll through Butchart Gardens, a short drive outside the city.

Shore Excursions

The following are good choices in Victoria. They may not be offered by all cruise lines. All times and prices are approximate.

Grand City Drive and Afternoon High Tea. This is a good choice for Anglophiles and others with an interest in Victoria's British heritage. The drive through downtown, past Craigdarroch Castle and residential areas, finishes with a British-style high tea at a hotel. A variation of this excursion takes visitors on a tour of the castle in lieu of high tea. *3½ hrs. Cost: $35.*

Short City Tour and Butchart Gardens. Drive through key places of interest, such as the city center and residential areas, on the way to Butchart Gardens—a must for garden aficionados. *3½ hrs. Cost: $39.*

Coming Ashore

Only the smallest excursion vessels can dock downtown in the Inner Harbour. Ocean liners must tie up at the Ogden Point Cruise Ship Terminal, a C$4–C$5 cab ride from downtown. Metered taxis meet the ship. The tourist visitor information center (812 Wharf St., tel. 250/953–2033) is in front of the Empress Hotel, midway along the Inner Harbour.

Most points of interest are within walking distance of the Empress Hotel. For those that aren't, public and private transportation is readily available from the Inner Harbour. The public bus system is excellent as well. Pick up route maps and schedules at the tourist information office.

BY TAXI

Rates are C$2.15 for pickup, C$1.30 per km (½ mi). Contact **Bluebird** (tel. 250/382–2222) or **Victoria Taxi** (250/383–7111).

Exploring Victoria

Numbers in the margin correspond to points of interest on the Inner Harbour, Victoria, map. Prices are given in Canadian dollars.

❶ Victoria's heart is the **Inner Harbour,** always bustling with ferries, seaplanes, and yachts from all over the world. The ivy-covered Empress Hotel (721 Government St., tel. 250/384–8111), with its well-groomed gardens, is the dowager of Victoria. High tea in this little patch of England is a local ritual: Recline in deep armchairs and nibble on scones or crumpets with honey, butter, jam, and clotted cream while sipping blended tea.

❷ The **Crystal Gardens** were built in 1925 under a glass roof as a public saltwater swimming pool. They have been renovated into a tropical conservatory and aviary, with flamingos, parrots, fountains, and waterfalls. *Douglas St. behind the Empress Hotel, tel. 250/381–1213. Admission: $7. Open spring and summer, daily 8–8; fall, daily 9–6.*

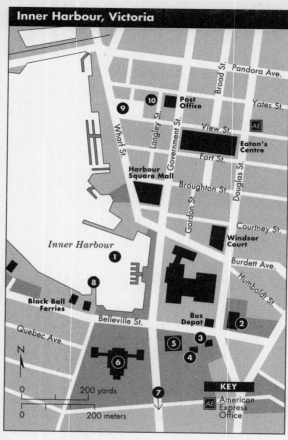

Inner Harbour, Victoria

Bastion
Square, **9**

British
Columbia
Parliament
Buildings, **6**

Crystal
Gardens, **2**

Emily Carr
House, **7**

Helmcken
House, **4**

Inner
Harbour, **1**

Maritime
Museum of
British
Columbia, **10**

Pacific
Underseas
Gardens, **8**

Royal British
Columbia
Museum, **5**

Thunderbird
Park, **3**

❸ **Thunderbird Park** displays a ceremonial longhouse (a communal dwelling) and the finest collection of replicated totem poles outside Alaska. *Belleville St.*

❹ Next to Thunderbird Park is **Helmcken House,** the province's oldest residence, which has a display of antique medical instruments. *10 Elliot St. Sq., tel. 250/361–0021. Admission: $4. Open daily 10–5.*

❺ The superb **Royal British Columbia Museum** will require at least an hour of your time: Its exhibits encompass 12,000 years of natural and human history. *675 Belleville St., tel. 250/387–3014. Admission: $5.35. Open summer, daily 9–7.*

❻ The stately, neo-Gothic **British Columbia Parliament Buildings** (501 Belleville St.) were constructed of local stone and wood and opened in 1898. Atop the central dome is a gilded statue of Captain George Vancouver, for whom Vancouver Island is named.

❼ Prints by Emily Carr, who was a member of the "Canadian Group of Seven," adorn the walls at the **Emily Carr House,** the beautifully restored residence of the famous early 20th-century painter. *207 Government St., tel. 250/383–5843. Admission: $4.50. Open May–Oct., daily 10–5.*

❽ You can descend beneath the water for a live scuba show with Armstrong, the Pacific octopus, at the **Pacific Underseas Gardens,** a natural aquarium with more than 5,000 species from the area. *490 Belleville St., tel. 250/382–5717. Admission: $7. Open summer, daily 9–9.*

❾ Just a short walk from the Inner Harbour is **Bastion Square.** Follow Government Street to Humboldt Street. With the water to your left, bear left onto Wharf Street, and look for the square on your right. Established in 1843 as the original site of Ft. Victoria, it now boasts several restored buildings open for viewing.

❿ On the far side of Bastion Square, the old courthouse is now the **Maritime Museum of British Columbia.** It has a collection of artifacts—including a 38-ft Native American dugout canoe and the 20-ft ketch *Trekka,* which has sailed around the world. In the Captain Cook gallery, nautical maps and other tools of 17th-century exploration are on display. *28 Bastion Sq., tel. 250/385–4222. Admission: $5. Open daily 9:30–4:30.*

Take a taxi (or a shore excursion) to **Butchart Gardens.** In a city of gardens, these 50 acres rank among the most beautiful in the world. In July and August, a fireworks display is held every Saturday evening. *22 km (14 mi) north of Victoria on Hwy. 17, tel. 250/652–4422. Admission: $15.50. Open daily at 9 AM–10:30 PM in summer.*

Shopping

Save your receipts to receive a 7% GST tax refund from the Canadian government when you leave Canada; ask for a form at customs. Victoria stores specializing in English imports are plentiful, though Canadian-made goods are usually a better buy for foreigners. Look for Hudson's Bay Co. blankets and other woolens. From the Empress Hotel walk along Government Street to reach **Piccadilly Shoppe British Woolens** and **Sasquatch Trading Company,** both of which sell high-quality woolen clothing.

Turn right onto Fort Street and walk four blocks to **Antique Row,** between Blanshard and Cook streets. The **Connoisseurs Shop** and **David Robinson, Ltd.** offer a wide variety of 18th-century pieces.

Dining

$$ **Bengal Lounge.** Buffet lunches in the elegant Empress Hotel include curries with extensive condiment trays of coconut, nuts, cool *raita* (yogurt with mint or cucumber), and chutney. Popular with cabinet ministers and bureaucrats, the Bengal Lounge offers splendid garden views. *721 Government St., tel. 250/384–8111. AE, D, DC, MC, V.*

$$ **La Ville d'Is.** This cozy and friendly seafood house, run by Brittany native Michel Duteau, is one of the best bargains in Victoria. The chef's strong suit is seafood, including lobster soufflé and *perche de la Nouvelle Aelande* (orange roughy in muscadet with herbs), rabbit, lamb, and beef tenderloin are also available. The wine list is limited but imaginative. On warm days there's seating outside. *26 Bastion Sq., tel. 250/388–9414. AE, DC, MC, V. Open for lunch and dinner Mon.-Fri., and for dinner only on Sat., closed Sun.*

Wrangell

Between Ketchikan and Petersburg lies Wrangell, on an island near the mouth of the fast-flowing Stikine River. The town is off the typical cruise-ship track and is visited mostly by lines with an environmental or educational emphasis, such as Alaska Sightseeing or World Explorer Cruises. A small, unassuming timber and fishing community, it has lived under three flags since the arrival of the Russian traders. Known as Redoubt St. Dionysius when it was part of Russian America, the town was renamed Fort Stikine after the British took it over. The name was changed to Wrangell when the Americans purchased it in 1867.

Shore Excursions

The following are good choices in Wrangell. They may not be offered by all cruise lines. All times and prices are approximate.

ISLAND SIGHTS

City Tour. Explore Native history at Shakes Island, the Wrangell Museum, and Petroglyph Beach. *2 hrs. Cost: $26.*

Stikine River Tour. Experience a thrilling jet-boat ride to the Stikine River. Visit Shakes Glacier, traveling in and around the icebergs, explore the back-slough and clear-water tributaries and listen to tales of gold-mining and fur trapping. *4 hrs. Cost: $140–$150.*

Coming Ashore

Cruise ships calling in Wrangell dock downtown, within walking distance of the museum and gift stores. Greeters welcome passengers and are available to answer questions. The chamber of commerce visitor center is next to the dock inside the Stikine Inn.

Wrangell's few attractions—most notably its totem park—is within walking distance of the pier. To get to Petroglyph Beach (*see* Exploring, *below*), where you find rocks marked with mysterious prehistoric symbols, you'll need to take a shore excursion or hire a cab. Call **Porky's Cab Co.** (tel. 907/874–3603) or **Star Cab** (tel. 907/874–3622).

Exploring Wrangell

Numbers in the margin correspond to points of interest on the Wrangell map.

❶ Walking up Front Street will bring you to **Kiksadi Totem Park,** a pocket park of Alaska greenery and impressive totem poles. This is the spot for a pleasant stroll.

❷ On your way to Wrangell's number-one attraction—Chief Shakes Island—stop at **Chief Shakes's grave site,** uphill from the Wrangell shipyard on Case Avenue. Buried here is Shakes VI, the last of a succession of chiefs who bore that name. He led the local Tlingits during the first half of the 19th century. Two killer-whale totems mark the chief's burial place.

❸ On **Chief Shakes Island,** reached by a footbridge off the harbor dock, you can see some of the finest totem poles in Alaska, as well as a tribal house constructed in the 1930s as a replica of one that was home to many of the various Shakes and their peoples. You'll see six totems on the island, two of them more than 100 years old. The original corner posts of the tribal house are in the museum. The house is open for visitors when ships are in port. *Tel. 907/874–2023 or 907/874–3747. Admission: $1 donation requested.*

❹ ❺ After your visit to Chief Shakes Island, wander out to the end of the dock for the view and for picture taking at the **seaplane float** and **boat harbor.**

❻ The **Wrangell City Museum's** historical collection includes totem fragments, petroglyphs, and other Native artifacts; a bootlegger's still; a vintage 1800s Linotype and presses; and a cedar-bark basket collection. *318 Church St., tel. 907/874–3770. Admission: $2. Open summer weekdays 10–5, Sat. 1–5, and, when cruise ships are in port.*

❼ Outside the **public library** (124 2nd Ave., tel. 907/874–3535) are a couple of ancient petroglyphs. It's worth seeing if you don't plan to make the trip to Petroglyph Beach (*see below*).

❽ To some, the artifacts that make up **"Our Collections"** by owner Elva Bigelow constitute less a museum than a garage sale waiting to happen. Still, large numbers of viewers seem quite taken by the literally thousands of unrelated collectibles (clocks, animal traps, waffle irons, tools, etc.) that the Bigelows have gathered in a half century of Alaska living. *Evergreen Ave., tel. 907/874–3646. Admission: Donations accepted. Call before setting out to visit.*

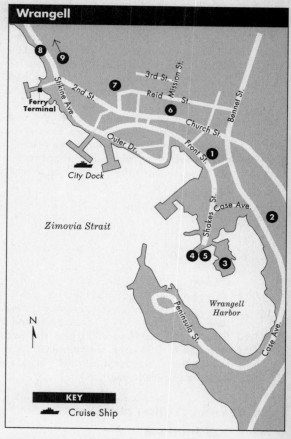

Wrangell

Zimovia Strait

Wrangell Harbor

3rd St.

Mission St.

Reid

2nd St.

Stikine Ave.

Church St.

Bennet St.

Front St.

Outer Dr.

Shakes St.

Case Ave.

Peninsula St.

Case Ave.

Ferry Terminal

City Dock

N

KEY

Cruise Ship

❾ **Petroglyph Beach** is undoubtedly one of the more curious
sights in Southeast Alaska. Here, scattered among other rocks
along the shore, are three dozen or more large stones bear-
ing designs and pictures chiseled by unknown ancient
artists. No one knows why the rocks were etched the way
they were. Perhaps they were boundary markers or mes-
sages; possibly they were just primitive doodling. Because
the petroglyphs can be damaged by physical contact, the
state discourages visitors from creating a "rubbing" off the
rocks with rice paper and crayons. Instead, you can photograph the petroglyphs or purchase a rubber-stamp dupli-
cate of selected petroglyphs from the city museum. Do not,
of course, attempt to move any of the petroglyph stones.

Shopping
A unique souvenir from Wrangell is a natural garnet, gathered at Garnet Ledge, facing the Stikine River. The semi-
precious gems are sold on the streets by the children of
Wrangell for 50¢ to $50, depending on their size and
quality.

Dining
$ Wrangell's dining options are limited, with no real stand-
outs. Several local restaurants, including the **Stikine Inn** (107
Front St., tel. 907/874–3388) and **Diamond C Cafe** (214
Front St., tel. 907/874–3677), offer standard fill-you-up
American fare. The best bet for visitors is probably **Waterfront Grill** (214 Front St., tel. 907/874–2353) for home-
made pizzas, salads, and burgers.

Ports of Embarkation and Disembarkation

San Francisco
The entire dock area of San Francisco is a tourist neighborhood of entertainment, shops, and restaurants called the
Embarcadero. There's plenty to see and do within easy walking distance of the cruise ship terminals. With your back
to the cruise pier, turn right to get to Fisherman's Wharf,
Ghirardelli Square, and the Maritime Museum. If you don't
want to walk, Bus 32 travels along the Embarcadero. You
can also pick up a ferry to Alcatraz at Pier 41.

LONG-TERM PARKING

A five-story public garage is one block from the cruise terminal at Pier 35. Parking is $8 per day.

FROM THE AIRPORT

San Francisco International Airport, one of the busiest in the country, is about 14 mi (22 km) from the cruise pier. A cab ride from the airport to the cruise pier costs a flat rate of $34 and takes 25–30 minutes, depending upon traffic. Less expensive ($12 per person) shuttle buses and shared stretch limousines can be picked up curbside at the airport, but they take longer. Make sure the shuttle or limousine will drop you off at the cruise pier.

Vancouver

Many travelers consider British Columbia's Vancouver one of the most beautiful cities in the world, so it is only appropriate that its cruise ship terminal is also one of the most convenient and attractive. Right on the downtown waterfront, the Canada Place terminal is instantly recognizable by its rooftop of dramatic sails. Inside are shops and restaurants. Porters are courteous and taxis plentiful.

If you are early, consider visiting historic Gastown just a couple of blocks away (to the left if you have your back to the water).

LONG-TERM PARKING

Parking at **Citipark** (tel. 604/684–2251 for reservations) at Canada Place costs C$14 per day for cruise ship passengers who pay in advance. Cheaper rates (less than C$10 a day) are available at certain hotels near the terminal, but you will need to take a cab between your car and the ship.

FROM THE AIRPORT

Vancouver International Airport is approximately 17½ km (11 mi) away from Canada Place, but the road weaves through residential neighborhoods instead of highways. A taxi from the airport costs about C$25 and takes about 25 minutes.

Cruise-line bus transfers from the Vancouver and Seattle airports are the most convenient, providing baggage handling and, for those with flights into Seattle, customs clearance. If for some reason you cannot connect with one of these buses, **Vancouver Airporter Service** (tel. 604/244–9888 or 800/668–3141) provides fast, frequent bus service between the Vancouver airport and the Pan Pacific Hotel at Canada Place for C$10 one-way, C$17 round-trip. From Seattle's SeaTac Airport, **Quick Shuttle** (tel. 604/244–3744 or 800/665–2122) makes the four- to five-hour bus trip for $35 one-way, $63 round-trip.

3 The Alaska Cruise Fleet

The Alaska cruise fleet is diverse: Of the more than 30 ships deployed in 1999, there are 19 ocean liners, two expedition ships, and 13 coastal cruisers. Passenger capacities range from nearly 2,000 people to fewer than a dozen. Lifestyle aboard these ships also spans the range, from formal to semiformal to casual. Three ships will be making their Alaska debut this year.

Ocean Liners

Classic Liners

CASUAL

Universe Explorer. World Explorer Cruises' strong suit is education, and passengers should not expect the glitz and glamour of some newer ships. The line's vessel (formerly the *Enchanted Seas* of Commodore Cruise Line) was built as a transatlantic liner, but World Explorer has modified it to serve as a floating classroom. Rather than the disco and casino typically found on cruise ships, the *Universe Explorer* has a herbarium and a 15,000-volume library—the largest at sea. Several other public rooms include a forward observation lounge. The *Universe Explorer*'s itinerary incorporates long port stays and an excellent array of shore excursions. On any given sailing, you may travel in the company of four or five experts in history, art, geology, marine life, music, or geography. Cabins are simple and spacious. *World Explorer Cruises, 555 Montgomery St., San Francisco, CA 94111, tel. 415/393–1565 or 800/854–3835. Built: 1958. Size: 23,500 tons. Capacity: 739 passengers. International officers and crew. 4 bars, 5 lounges, fitness center with massage, cinema, card room, library, youth center. Cabin amenities: Color TV. Average per diem: $200–$300.*

Cruise Liners

FORMAL

Crystal Harmony. The *Crystal Harmony* is exceptionally sleek and sophisticated. Spacious and well equipped, the ship has plenty of open deck space for watching the scenery plus a forward observation lounge with oversize windows, set high above the bridge. Unlike most ships in this price category, the *Harmony* serves dinner in the main dining room in two seatings. Passengers may choose to dine in the alternative Asian or Italian restaurant at no extra charge. Cabins are especially spacious; more than half have a private veranda. *Crystal Cruises, 2121 Avenue of the Stars, Los Angeles, CA 90067, tel. 310/785–9300 or 800/446–6620. Built: 1990. Size: 49,400 tons. Capacity: 940 passengers. Norwegian and Japanese officers and an international crew. 7 bars, 6 entertainment lounges, fitness center with massage and sauna, casino, cinema, library, video arcade, smoking room. Cabin amenities: 24-hr room service, refrigerator, robes, TV-VCR. Average per diem: $400–$500.*

SEMIFORMAL

Nieuw Amsterdam and **Noordam.** More traditionally styled than the newest and snazziest ships, these ships both carry aboard a multimillion-dollar collection of 17th- and 18th-century antiques. About the only difference between these identical sisters is the theme of their art: Dutch exploration in the New World aboard the *Nieuw Amsterdam* and in the Old World on the *Noordam.* Unlike their newer sisters, these mid-size ships have smaller outside deck areas, tiny gyms, and one-level dining rooms, although outside staterooms are spacious. Tipping is optional, but passengers tend to tip anyway. A resident naturalist sails aboard each Alaska cruise, and the Passport to Fitness Program encourages a healthy diet and exercise. *Holland America Line Westours, 300 Elliott Ave. W, Seattle, WA 98119, tel. 206/281–3535 or 800/426–0327. Built: 1983/1984. Size: 33,930 tons. Capacity: 1,214 passengers. Dutch officers and Indonesian and Filipino crew. 7 bars, 3 entertainment lounges, fitness center with massage and sauna, casino, cinema, video-game room, library. Cabin amenities: 24-hr room service, TV. Average per diem: $400–$500.*

Ryndam, Statendam, and **Veedam.** These ships can best be described as classic-revival, combining the old and new in one neat package. From the outside, they look bigger than their 55,000 tons, thanks to their megaship profile. Inside, they dramatically express Holland America's past in a two-tier dining room, replete with dual grand staircases framing an orchestra balcony—the latter first introduced on the *Nieuw Amsterdam* of 1938. Although the ships are structurally identical, Holland America has given each its own distinct personality in the layout and decor of the public rooms. An abundance of glass, outdoor deck space, and a retractable roof over the main pool make these good ships for Alaska cruising. Great views can be found along the wraparound promenade, from the top-deck observation lounge, and during meals in the glass-lined dining room. All standard outside cabins come with a small sitting area and a real tub; some have private verandas. Tipping is optional, but passengers tend to tip anyway. A resident naturalist sails aboard each Alaska cruise, and the Passport to Fitness Program encourages a healthy diet and exercise. *Holland America Line Westours, 300 Elliott Ave. W, Seattle, WA 98119, tel. 206/281–3535 or 800/426–0327. Built: 1994/1993/1993. Size: 55,451 tons. Capacity: 1,266 passengers. Dutch officers and Indonesian and Filipino crew. 5 lounges, 7 bars, fitness center with massage and sauna, casino, cinema. Cabin amenities: 24-hr room service, TV. Average per diem: $400–$500.*

Sky Princess. This ship combines an old-liner atmosphere with the modern touches passengers expect from a cruise ship. The showroom is one of the biggest afloat and public spaces are appointed with a notable collection of contemporary art. Most public rooms command good views of the sea. The Horizon Lounge, for example, offers floor-to-ceiling windows and a view directly over the bow—perfect for sailing in scenic waters. The two dining rooms are of intimate size, identical in decor, and have windows that provide a reasonably good view of the passing scene. Cabins are spacious. Suites have verandas and bathtubs. *Princess Cruises, 10100 Santa Monica Blvd., Los Angeles, CA 90067, tel. 310/553–1770 or 800/568–3262. Built: 1984. Size: 46,314 tons. Capacity: 1,200 passengers. British officers and European hotel crew. 7 bars, 4 entertainment lounges, fitness center with massage and sauna, library, youth and teen centers. Cabin amenities: 24-hr room service, robes, TV. Average per diem: $400–$500.*

Westerdam. As with other Holland America ships, the *Westerdam* carries a multimillion-dollar art collection that evokes the cruise line's storied history. Perhaps most impressive is an antique bronze cannon, cast in Rotterdam, which is strategically positioned in the center of the ship.

Also worthy of special note is the dining room. Unlike on many newer ships, where the restaurant occupies a strategic perch with expansive views, on the *Westerdam* it is located below decks. But Holland America has turned a negative into a positive; the room is attractively accented with wood and brass, and traditional portholes. Cabins are large, with plenty of storage space; all but the least expensive feature a sitting area with a convertible couch. Tipping is optional, but passengers tend to tip anyway. A resident naturalist sails aboard each Alaska cruise, and the Passport to Fitness Program encourages exercise and a healthy diet. *Holland America Line Westours, 300 Elliott Ave. W, Seattle, WA 98119, tel. 206/281–3535 or 800/426–0327. Built: 1986. Size: 53,872 tons. Capacity: 1,494 passengers. Dutch officers and Indonesian and Filipino crew. 7 bars, 2 entertainment lounges, fitness center with massage and sauna, casino, cinema, video-game room, library. Cabin amenities: 24-hr room service, TV. Average per diem: $400–$500.*

CASUAL

Jubilee. The *Jubilee* brings Carnival's "Fun Ship" style of cruising to the Last Frontier. The ship offers plenty of open space and has many resortlike qualities, although, the *Jubilee* is not nearly as sharp and state-of-the-art as Carnival's newer vessels. The interior is modern and festive, spanning the entire spectrum of colors. Cabins are of similar size and appearance, comfortable and larger than average; the majority have twin beds that can be made into a king-size bed. Most outside cabins have large square windows rather than portholes. *Carnival Cruise Lines, Carnival Pl., 3655 N.W. 87th Ave., Miami, FL 33178, tel. 800/327–9501. Built: 1986. Size: 47,262 tons. Capacity: 1,486 passengers. Italian officers and an international crew. 7 bars, 6 entertainment lounges, fitness center with massage and sauna, casino, video-game room, library, playroom. Cabin amenities: 24-hr room service, TV. Average per diem: $200–$300.*

Megaships
SEMIFORMAL

Crown Princess and **Regal Princess.** These identical sisters are unmistakable because of the white dome that tops each ship. Underneath is a 13,000-square-ft entertainment and

observation area with 270-degree views—perfect for a
rainy day in Glacier Bay. A small observation deck below
the bridge gives great views and you'll likely have it all to
yourself: It's so well-hidden, it's not even on the deck plan.
There's a ⅙-mi tractioned outdoor running track, and the
ships carry an impressive contemporary art collection. Cabins are quite spacious, and suites, minisuites, and some standard cabins have private verandas. *Princess Cruises, 10100
Santa Monica Blvd., Los Angeles, CA 90067, tel. 310/
553–1770 or 800/568–3262. Built: 1990/1991. Size:
70,000 tons. Capacity: 1,590 passengers. Italian officers and
international crew. 9 bars, 5 entertainment lounges, fitness
center with massage and sauna, casino, cinema, library.
Cabin amenities: 24-hr room service, refrigerator, robes, TV.
Average per diem: $400–$500.*

Galaxy and **Mercury.** With features like video walls and interactive television systems in cabins, both ships are high-
tech pioneers, yet at the same time elegant, warm, well-
appointed. For example, the ships' spas are some of the best
at sea. The ships' many large windows (including a dramatic
two-story wall of glass in the dining room and wraparound
windows in the Stratosphere Lounge, the gym, and beauty
salon) and glass sunroofs over their pools bathe the ship
in natural light and afford excellent viewing of Alaska's natural beauty. *Celebrity Cruises, 5200 Blue Lagoon Dr.,
Miami, FL 33126, tel. 800/437–3111. Built: 1996/1997.
Size: 77,713. Capacity: 1,870 passengers. Greek officers and
international crew. 11 bar-lounges, golf simulator, health
club with massage and sauna, thalassotherapy pool, casino,
video-game room, library, playroom. Cabin amenities: 24-
hr room service, butler service in suites, minibar, TV. Average per diem: $400–$500.*

Sea Princess, **Dawn Princess,** and **Sun Princess.** The brand-
new *Sea Princess,* and its sisters, the *Dawn Princess* and
Sun Princess, offer the greatest number of private balconies
(more than 70% of outside cabins have them) of any ships
sailing in Alaska. Each has two main show rooms and two
main passenger dining rooms; an international food court
with a 270-degree view over the bow of the ship; an Ital-
ian-style pizzeria; a wine and caviar bar; and a patisserie
for coffee and drinks. *Princess Cruises, 10100 Santa Mon-*

ica Blvd., Los Angeles, CA 90067, tel. 310/553–1770 or 800/568–3262. Built: 1995/1997/1998. Size: 77,000 tons. Capacity: 1,950 passengers. Italian and British officers and European, American, and Filipino crew. 7 bars, 2 entertainment lounges, fitness center with massage and sauna, basketball court, golf simulator, casino, library, teen and children's center. Cabin amenities: 24-hr room service, refrigerator, robes, TV. Average per diem: $500–$600.

CASUAL

Vision of the Seas and **Rhapsody of the Seas.** The brand new *Vision* and the *Rhapsody* have dramatic balconied dining rooms and tiered showrooms. For great views of the passing scenery, each ship has a "Viking Crown Lounge" on the uppermost deck with wraparound glass. The indoor/outdoor deck area in the Solarium Spas are especially well suited for cruising in often rainy Alaska. The *Rhapsody* and *Vision* have relatively large cabins and more balconies than Royal Caribbean's previous megaships. Of the total cabins aboard, about one quarter have private verandas. The ships also have specially designed family suites with separate bedrooms for parents and children. *Royal Caribbean Cruise Line, 1050 Caribbean Way, Miami, FL 33132, tel. 800/327–6700 (reservations) or 800/255–4373 (brochures). Built: 1997/ 1998. Size: 78,491 tons. Capacity: 2,000 passengers. Norwegian officers and international staff. 8 bars, 3 lounges, fitness center with massage and sauna, casino, theater, library, youth center. Cabin amenities: 24-hr room service, TV. Average per diem: $300–$400.*

Small Ships

Expedition Ships

CASUAL

Hanseatic. The *Hanseatic* is the world's newest, biggest, and most luxurious expedition ship. Its passenger-to-crew ratio rivals the standards of the world's most expensive ships. And due to its size, there is a varied selection of public rooms. A top-deck observation lounge with 180-degree views offers comfortable, all-weather sightseeing; there's also a glass-enclosed whirlpool. A team of experts, such as naturalists and marine biologists, brief passengers in the Darwin Lounge, a state-of-the-art facility with video and sound systems. (You can also watch the lectures in your cabin.) The experts then accompany passengers ashore. Cabins are unusually spacious, and all have outside views and sitting areas. The ship is popular with Europeans. *Radisson Seven Seas Cruises, 600 Corporate Dr., Suite 410, Fort Lauderdale, FL 33334, tel. 800/333–3333. Built: 1993. Size: 9,000 tons. Capacity: 188 passengers. European officers and international crew. 2 lounge-bars, fitness center with massage and sauna, cinema, library. Cabin amenities: Refrigerator, TV, VCR, tub. Average per diem: $600–$700.*

World Discoverer. This true expedition vessel, with a shallow draft and ice-hardened hull, is well equipped for Zodiac landings in intriguing ports of call. Naturalists and other guest lecturers enhance the shoreside experience and give enrichment talks in the theater. Cabins are small, but all are outside. Fares include all shore excursions except flightseeing. *Society Expeditions, 2001 Western Ave., Suite 300, Seattle, WA 98121, tel. 800/548–8669. Built: 1974. Size: 3,724 tons. Capacity: 138 passengers. German and Filipino officers, European and Filipino crew, international cruise and lecturer staff. 2 bars, 2 lounges, small gym and sauna, observation lounge, cinema–lecture hall, library. Average per diem: $400–$500.*

Coastal Cruisers

CASUAL

Executive Explorer. As the name suggests, the Executive Explorer is a plush ship. Its appointments include rich wood paneling throughout, deep-padded armchairs in the main lounge, and a gallery-like display of nearly 100 Alaskan prints. The main lounge has forward-facing observation windows; the dining room has color TV monitors. Even the stairwells have picture windows for views of the passing scenery. Outside observation areas include a partially covered sundeck, which gives a lofty perspective four decks above the water—an unusually high perch for such a small ship. Cabins have more artwork, two more big picture windows (unusually large for a ship this size), roomy closets, and other cabin amenities not often found in small-ship cabins. *Glacier Bay Tours and Cruises, 520 Pike St., Suite 1400, Seattle, WA 98101, tel. 800/451–5952 (U.S. and Canada). Built: 1986. Size: 98 tons. Capacity: 49 passen-*

gers. *American officers and crew. Observation lounge. Cabin amenities: Minibar, refrigerator, color TV, VCR. Average per diem: $400–$500.*

Sea Bird and **Sea Lion.** These small shallow-draft ships have the freedom to sail through narrow straits and visit out-of-the-way areas that are inaccessible to big ships. The boats forgo port calls at larger, busier towns and instead spend time making Zodiac raft landings, conducting wildlife searches, and stopping for beachcombing and barbecuing in Tracy Arm. These ships are not for claustrophobics, as the ship's storage capacity, the size of the crews, and the number of public areas have been cut back in order to carry 70 passengers. All cabins are technically outside staterooms, but Category 1 rooms have only a high port light (a very small porthole). *Special Expeditions, 720 5th Ave., New York, NY 10019, tel. 212/765–7740 or 800/762–0003. Built: 1982/1981. Size: 100 tons. Capacity: 70 passengers. American officers and crew. Bar-lounge, library. Average per diem: $500–$600.*

Spirit of Alaska. Alaska Sightseeing's original overnight vessel is still its coziest. You are never by yourself in the lounge, and meals in the homey dining room resemble a family affair soon after the cruise has begun. Sleek and small, the *Spirit of Alaska* feels like a real yacht. A bow ramp adds to the sense of adventure, allowing passengers to put ashore at tiny islands and beaches few other cruise travelers visit. Toilets and showers are a combined unit (meaning that the toilet is inside the shower). Suites and some outside cabins have TVs, but only for watching videos. *Alaska Sightseeing/Cruise West, 4th & Battery Bldg., Suite 700, Seattle, WA 98121, tel. 206/441–8687 or 800/426–7702. Built: 1980; refurbished: 1991. Size: 97 tons. Capacity: 82 passengers. American/Canadian officers and crew. Bar-lounge, exercise equipment. Average per diem: $400–$500.*

Spirit of Columbia. Although cut from the same mold as Alaska Sightseeing's *Spirit of Alaska,* this ship has one notable feature: a unique bow ramp design that allows passengers to walk directly from the forward lounge onto shore. The interior design was inspired by the national-park lodges of the American West, with a color scheme based on muted shades of evergreen, rust, and sand. All suites and deluxe cabins have a mini-refrigerator, an armchair and a small desk. The Owner's Suite stretches the width of the vessel; located just under the bridge, its row of forward-facing windows gives a captain's-eye view of the ship's progress. Suites and deluxe cabins have TVs, but only for watching videos. *Alaska Sightseeing/Cruise West, 4th & Battery Bldg., Suite 700, Seattle, WA 98121, tel. 206/441–8687 or 800/426–7702. Built: 1979; refurbished: 1994. Size: 98 tons. Capacity: 81 passengers. American/Canadian officers and crew. Bar-lounge, exercise equipment. Average per diem: $400–$500.*

Spirit of Discovery. Floor-to-ceiling windows in the main lounge provide stunning views of passing scenery for passengers aboard this snazzy cruiser. Blue-suede chairs, a wraparound bench sofa at the bow, and a mirrored ceiling make the chrome-filled lounge look especially swank. From here, passengers have direct access to a large outdoor viewing deck, one of two aboard. This is great for those who don't want to trudge upstairs every time a whale is spotted. Deluxe cabins have mini-refrigerator, two cabins are reserved for single travelers, and many cabins have extra large picture windows. Toilets and showers are a combined unit (meaning that the toilet is inside the shower). Suites and some outside cabins have TVs, but only for watching videos. *Alaska Sightseeing/Cruise West, 4th & Battery Bldg., Suite 700, Seattle, WA 98121, tel. 206/441–8687 or 800/426–7702. Built: 1976. Size: 94 tons. Capacity: 84 passengers. American/Canadian officers and crew. Bar-lounge, exercise equipment. Cabin amenities: Refrigerator and TV-VCR in deluxe cabins. Average per diem: $400–$500.*

Spirit of Endeavour. Alaska Sightseeing's newest flagship is also the line's largest. Oak and teak are used throughout the light and airy ship. All cabins are outside with large picture windows for superb views. Some cabins have connecting doors, which make them convenient for families traveling together, and all cabins have TVs and VCRs, but only for watching videos. *Alaska Sightseeing/Cruise West, 4th & Battery Bldg., Suite 700, Seattle, WA 98121, tel. 206/441–8687 or 800/426–7702. Built: 1984; refurbished: 1996. Size: 99 tons. Capacity: 107 passengers. American/Canadian officers and crew. Bar, lounge, library.*

Cabin amenities: TV-VCR in all cabins and refrigerator in some. Average per diem: 500–$600.

Spirit of Glacier Bay. Alaska Sightseeing's smallest overnight cruiser is nearly identical to the line's *Spirit of Alaska,* and its public rooms are even cozier. Wraparound couches and small table-and-chair groupings in the lounge create a living-room feel. Cabins on the lowest deck have no window, just a high port light, but soft, cream-color fabrics help brighten up the ship's tiny accommodations. Toilets and showers are a combined unit (meaning that the toilet is inside the shower). There are no TVs in any cabins. *Alaska Sightseeing/Cruise West, 4th & Battery Bldg., Suite 700, Seattle, WA 98121, tel. 206/441–8687 or 800/426–7702. Built: 1971. Size: 98 tons. Capacity: 52 passengers. American/Canadian officers and crew. Bar-lounge. Average per diem: $400–$500.*

Spirit of '98. With its rounded stern and wheelhouse, old-fashioned smokestack, and Victorian decor, the *Spirit of '98* evokes the feel of a turn-of-the-century steamer. Inside and out, mahogany adorns this elegant ship. Overstuffed chairs upholstered in crushed velvet complete the gold-rush-era motif. For private moments, there are plenty of nooks and crannies aboard the ship, along with the cozy Soapy's Parlor at the stern, with a small bar and a few tables and chairs. All cabins are outside with picture windows, and have TVs, but only for watching videos. *Alaska Sightseeing/Cruise West, 4th & Battery Bldg., Suite 700, Seattle, WA 98121, tel. 206/441–8687 or 800/426–7702. Built: 1984; refurbished: 1993. Size: 96 tons. Capacity: 101 passengers. American/Canadian officers and crew. 2 bar-lounges, exercise equipment. Average per diem: $400–$500.*

Wilderness Adventurer. This is a friendly ship with the casual comforts of home. The coffee's always on and you'll never need a jacket and tie for dinner. Alaskan art enhances the otherwise simple surroundings, and there's just enough varnished wood to imbue a nautical feel. A library of books and videos has a nice selection of Alaska titles. There are no TVs, but you can watch these tapes—or your own wildlife footage—on the community VCR in the main lounge. But the most important asset of this ship are its naturalists, who put their hearts into their work. They lead kayak excursions and shore walks, and get as much of a thrill as the passengers do whenever wildlife is sighted. Cabins, like the rest of the ship, are simple and functional. (The toilet and sink are in the shower.) *Glacier Bay Tours and Cruises, 520 Pike St., Suite 1400, Seattle, WA 98101, tel. 800/451–5952 (U.S. and Canada). Built: 1983. Size: 89 tons. Capacity: 74 passengers. American officers and crew. Observation lounge. Average per diem: $400–$500.*

Wilderness Discoverer. This latest addition to the Glacier Bay fleet was formerly American Canadian Caribbean Line's *Mayan Prince*. You can expect the same general ambience and genuine enthusiasm from the crew as you would find aboard the *Wilderness Adventurer* (*see above*) *Glacier Bay Tours and Cruises. 520 Pike St., Suite 1400, Seattle, WA 98101, tel. 800/451–5952 in U.S. and Canada. Built: 1992. Size: 98 tons. Capacity: 86 passengers. American officers and crew. Observation lounge. Average per diem: $400–$500.*

Wilderness Explorer. The Wilderness Explorer is billed as a "floating base camp" for "active adventure," and that's no exaggeration. Sea-kayak outings may last more than three hours (a 5-mi paddle). Discovery hikes cross dense thicket and climb rocky creek beds. You'll spend most of your time off the ship—which is a good thing, since you wouldn't want to spend much time on it. Decor-wise, the ship is pleasing enough—mostly late 1960s mod with a dash of old world leather and even Greek Revival accents. But the public spaces are very limited and the cabins are positively tiny. This ship is not for the typical cruise passenger, and should be considered only by the serious outdoor enthusiast. *Glacier Bay Tours and Cruises, 520 Pike St., Suite 1400, Seattle, WA 98101, tel. 800/451–5952 (U.S. and Canada). Built: 1969. Size: 98 tons. Capacity: 36 passengers. American officers and crew. Observation lounge. Average per diem: $300–$400.*

Yorktown Clipper. The *Yorktown Clipper* is a stylish coastal cruiser with a casual sophistication. There are only a few public rooms—which are bright and comfortable—and deck space is limited. Onboard naturalists and Zodiac landing craft enhance the emphasis on destination. Floor-to-ceiling windows in the lounge and large windows in the dining room allow sightseeing in all weather. Cabins are all outside, and most have large windows. The crew is young and enthusiastic. *Clipper Cruise Lines, 7711 Bonhomme Ave., St. Louis, MO 63105, tel. 314/727–2929 or 800/325–0010. Built: 1988. Size: 97 tons. Capacity: 138 passengers. American officers and crew. Bar-lounge. Average per diem: $300–$400.*

Special-Interest Cruises

The **Alaska Marine Highway** (Box 25535, Juneau, AK 99802, tel. 800/642–0066, fax 907/277–4829) has cabins aboard several ferries that serve the communities of southeast and south-central Alaska. Dining is cafeteria-style with good American-style food. Public rooms include an observation lounge, a bar, and a solarium. Many passengers are RV travelers transporting their vehicles (no roads connect the towns within the Inside Passage). Time spent in port is short—often just long enough to load and unload the ship. A weekly departure leaves from Bellingham, Washington, north of Seattle. Service to Alaska is also available from Prince Rupert, British Columbia, where the marine highway system connects with Canada's BC Ferries. Cabins on the Alaskan ferries book up as soon they become available, but a number of tour operators sell packages that include accommodations. One of the oldest and largest is Knightly Tours (Box 16366, Seattle, WA 98116, tel. 206/938–8567 or 800/426–2123, fax 206/938–8498).

Discovery Voyages (Box 1500, Cordova, AK 99574, tel. 907/472–2558) sails solely within Prince William Sound on the 12-passenger, 65-ft *Discovery,* which was built in the 1950s as a Presbyterian mission boat. To carry guests, the vessel has been completely renovated by owners Dean and Rose Rand, who live aboard the ship year-round. Passenger facilities include six cabins with shared baths and a main lounge/dining room. The ship is also equipped with inflatable skiffs and kayaks for off-ship excursions. Sailings are round-trip from Whittier, Cordova, or between Whittier and Cordova.

Another option for cruising Prince William Sound is the four-passenger *Arctic Tern III,* which is one of the smallest overnight vessels sailing in Alaska. Longtime Sound residents Jim and Nancy Lethcoe operate the boat under the name **Alaska Wilderness Sailing Safaris** (tel. 907/835–5175, fax 907/835–3765) and charter the 40-ft sloop to small parties of two to four passengers, generally for three days of sailing and kayaking.

A number of interesting and unorthodox cruise vessels travel the Inside Passage, too. For a cruise aboard a former minesweeper, contact the **Boat Company** (19623 Viking Ave. NW, Poulsbo, WA 98370, tel. 360/697–5454, fax 360/697–4213). The 12-passenger *Observer* and 20-passenger *Liseron* were commissioned by the Navy in the 1940s and 1950s, but are now in service to the conservation movement. In the past, organizations such as the Sierra Club have brought groups aboard, and all sailings are designed to raise awareness of environmental issues. The vessels themselves are constructed of wood and finished with accents of brass and bronze, so dismiss any thoughts of boats painted battleship gray.

Similar environmentally oriented programs can be found aboard the 16-passenger *Island Roamer,* a 68-ft sailboat operated by **Bluewater Adventures** (tel. 604/980–3800, fax 604/980–1800), which has been in business for more than 20 years. The vessel is sometimes chartered by Oceanic Society Expeditions, an affiliate of Friends of the Earth. Bluewater Adventures also has the 12-passenger *Snow Goose,* a 65-ft, steel-hulled motor yacht. Built in 1973, it too has served time as a research vessel. For leisure cruising, the *Snow Goose* has a Zodiac, two kayaks, and a natural-history library.

For something even smaller, **Dolphin Charters** (tel. 510/527–9622, fax 510/525–0720) uses the *Delphinus* (eight passengers), a 50-ft motor yacht, to explore uncharted coves throughout Southeast Alaska. This vessel is popular with professional photographers, who often hire it for their photographic workshops.

Equally intimate is the eight-passenger *Steller* from **Glacier Bay Adventures** (tel. 907/697–2442). The vessel was built as a research vessel for the Alaska Department of Fish and Game and is staffed by a crew of trained naturalists.

Outside of Glacier Bay, another cozy cruise for just six passengers at a time can be booked from **All Aboard Yacht Charters** (tel. 360/898–7300 or 888/801–9004, fax 360/898–7301). Cruises on the *Sea Play* sail from Seattle to Ketchikan, from Ketchikan to Juneau, and on loops round-trip from Juneau.

Alaska Sea Adventures (tel. 253/927–7147) caters to sport-fishing enthusiasts, photography buffs, and amateur naturalists aboard the *Alaska Adventurer*. The ship holds up to 10 passengers and was built in 1980 specifically for cruising the Inside Passage.

4 Itineraries

SAILING SCHEDULES

Itineraries are for the 1999 Alaska season aboard the top cruise lines, as described in *Fodor's The Best Cruises '99*. Ship deployments and itineraries are subject to change; ports of call may also vary with departure date. Check with your cruise line or travel agent.

Alaska Sightseeing/Cruise West

SPIRIT OF ALASKA

10-night **Inside Passage** cruise from Seattle to Juneau. 3- and 4-night **Prince William Sound** loops from Whittier.

SPIRIT OF COLUMBIA

12-night **Inside Passage** cruise from Seattle to Juneau. 7-night **Inside Passage** cruises between Juneau and Ketchikan.

SPIRIT OF DISCOVERY

7-night **Inside Passage** cruises between Juneau and Ketchikan.

SPIRIT OF ENDEAVOUR

7-night **Inside Passage** cruises between Seattle and Juneau.

SPIRIT OF GLACIER BAY

3- and 4-night **Prince William Sound** loops from Whittier.

SPIRIT OF '98

7-night **Inside Passage** cruises between Seattle and Juneau.

Alaska's Glacier Bay Tours & Cruises

WILDERNESS DISCOVERER

10-night **Inside Passage** cruises between Seattle and Juneau. 6-night **Alaska** cruises to be announced.

EXECUTIVE EXPLORER

9-night **Inside Passage** cruises between Seattle and Juneau. 7-night **Inside Passage** cruises between Ketchikan and Juneau.

WILDERNESS EXPLORER

10-night **Inside Passage** cruises between Seattle and Juneau. 3-, 4- and 5-night **Inside Passage** cruises from Juneau.

WILDERNESS ADVENTURER
10-night **Inside Passage** cruises between Seattle and Juneau.
6-night **Inside Passage** loops from Juneau.

Carnival Cruise Lines

JUBILEE
7-night **Inside Passage/Gulf of Alaska** cruises between
Vancouver and Seward (Alaska). 7-night **Inside Passage**
loops from Vancouver.

Celebrity Cruises

GALAXY
11-night **Inside Passage** cruise from Los Angeles to Vancouver. 7-night **Inside Passage** loops from Vancouver.

MERCURY
10-night **Inside Passage** cruise from Los Angeles to Vancouver. 7-night **Inside Passage** loop from Vancouver. 7-night
Inside Passage/Gulf of Alaska cruises between Vancouver
and Seward (Alaska).

Clipper Cruise Line

YORKTOWN CLIPPER
10- and 11-night **Inside Passage** cruises between Seattle and
Juneau. 7-night **Inside Passage** cruises between Juneau
and Ketchikan and loops from Juneau.

Crystal Cruises

CRYSTAL HARMONY
12-night **Inside Passage** loops from San Francisco.

Holland America Line

NIEUW AMSTERDAM
7-night **Inside Passage** loops from Vancouver.

NOORDAM
7-night **Inside Passage/Gulf of Alaska** cruises between Vancouver and Seward (Alaska). 7-night **Inside Passage** loops from Vancouver.

RYNDAM
7-night **Inside Passage/Gulf of Alaska** cruises between Vancouver and Seward (Alaska). 7-night **Inside Passage** loops from Vancouver.

STATENDAM
7-night **Inside Passage/Gulf of Alaska** cruises between Vancouver and Seward (Alaska). 7-night **Inside Passage** loops from Vancouver.

VEENDAM
7-night **Inside Passage** loops from Vancouver.

WESTERDAM
7-night **Inside Passage** loops from Vancouver.

Princess Cruises

CROWN PRINCESS
7-night **Inside Passage/Gulf of Alaska** cruises between Vancouver and Seward (Alaska).

DAWN PRINCESS
7-night **Inside Passage/Gulf of Alaska** cruises between Vancouver and Seward (Alaska).

REGAL PRINCESS
7-night **Inside Passage/Gulf of Alaska** cruises between Vancouver and Seward (Alaska).

SEA PRINCESS
7-night **Inside Passage/Gulf of Alaska** cruises between Vancouver and Seward (Alaska).

SKY PRINCESS
11-night **Inside Passage** loops from San Francisco.

SUN PRINCESS
7-night **Inside Passage** loops from Vancouver.

Radisson Seven Seas Cruises

HANSEATIC
Bering Sea cruises to be announced.

Royal Caribbean International

RHAPSODY OF THE SEAS
7-night **Inside Passage** loops from Vancouver.

VISION OF THE SEAS
7-night **Inside Passage** loops from Vancouver.

Society Expeditions

WORLD DISCOVERER
Bering Sea cruises to be announced.

Special Expeditions

SEA BIRD, SEA LION
7-night **Inside Passage** cruises between Juneau and Sitka.
10-night **Alaska/British Columbia** cruises between Juneau and Seattle.

World Explorer Cruises

UNIVERSE EXPLORER
14-night **Inside Passage** loops from Vancouver. 9-night **Inside Passage/Gulf of Alaska** loops from Vancouver.

INDEX

✕ = *restaurant*, 🏨 = *hotel*

NOTES

NOTES

NOTES

NOTES

NOTES

NOTES

NOTES

NOTES

NOTES

NOTES

Fodor's Travel Publications

Available at bookstores everywhere. For descriptions of all our titles, a key to Fodor's guidebook series, and on-line ordering, visit www.fodors.com/books

Gold Guides

U.S.

Alaska
Arizona
Boston
California
Cape Cod,
Martha's Vineyard,
Nantucket
The Carolinas &
Georgia
Chicago
Colorado

Florida
Hawai'i
Las Vegas, Reno,
Tahoe
Los Angeles
Maine, Vermont,
New Hampshire
Maui & Lāna'i
Miami & the Keys
New England
New Orleans

New York City
Oregon
Pacific North
Coast
Philadelphia & the
Pennsylvania
Dutch Country
The Rockies
San Diego
San Francisco

Santa Fe, Taos,
Albuquerque
Seattle &
Vancouver
The South
U.S. & British
Virgin Islands
USA
Virginia &
Maryland
Washington, D.C.

Foreign

Australia
Austria
The Bahamas
Belize &
Guatemala
Bermuda
Canada
Cancún, Cozumel,
Yucatán Peninsula
Caribbean
China
Costa Rica
Cuba
The Czech
Republic &
Slovakia
Denmark

Eastern &
Central Europe
Europe
Florence, Tuscany
& Umbria
France
Germany
Great Britain
Greece
Hong Kong
India
Ireland
Israel
Italy
Japan
London

Madrid &
Barcelona
Mexico
Montréal &
Québec City
Moscow,
St. Petersburg,
Kiev
The Netherlands,
Belgium &
Luxembourg
New Zealand
Norway
Nova Scotia, New
Brunswick, Prince
Edward Island
Paris
Portugal

Provence &
the Riviera
Scandinavia
Scotland
Singapore
South Africa
South America
Southeast Asia
Spain
Sweden
Switzerland
Thailand
Toronto
Turkey
Vienna & the
Danube Valley
Vietnam

Special-Interest Guides

Adventures to
Imagine
Alaska Ports of Call
Ballpark Vacations
The Best Cruises
Caribbean Ports
of Call
The Complete
Guide to America's
National Parks
Europe Ports of Call
Family Adventures
Fodor's Gay Guide
to the USA

Fodor's How to Pack
Great American
Learning Vacations
Great American
Sports & Adventure
Vacations
Great American
Vacations
Great American
Vacations
for Travelers
with Disabilities
Halliday's
New Orleans
Food Explorer

Healthy Escapes
Kodak Guide to
Shooting Great
Travel Pictures
National Parks
and Seashores
of the East
National Parks of
the West
Nights to Imagine
Orlando Like a Pro
Rock & Roll
Traveler Great
Britain and Ireland

Rock & Roll
Traveler USA
Sunday in San
Francisco
Walt Disney
World for Adults
Weekends in
New York
Wendy Perrin's
Secrets Every
Smart Traveler
Should Know
Worlds to Imagine

Fodor's Special Series

Fodor's Best Bed & Breakfasts
America
California
The Mid-Atlantic
New England
The Pacific Northwest
The South
The Southwest
The Upper Great Lakes

Compass American Guides
Alaska
Arizona
Boston
Chicago
Coastal California
Colorado
Florida
Hawai'i
Hollywood
Idaho
Las Vegas
Maine
Manhattan
Minnesota
Montana
New Mexico
New Orleans
Oregon
Pacific Northwest
San Francisco
Santa Fe
South Carolina
South Dakota
Southwest
Texas
Underwater Wonders of the National Parks
Utah
Virginia
Washington
Wine Country
Wisconsin
Wyoming

Citypacks
Amsterdam
Atlanta
Berlin
Boston
Chicago
Florence
Hong Kong
London
Los Angeles
Miami
Montréal
New York City
Paris
Prague
Rome

San Francisco
Sydney
Tokyo
Toronto
Venice
Washington, D.C.

Exploring Guides
Australia
Boston &
New England
Britain
California
Canada
Caribbean
China
Costa Rica
Cuba
Egypt
Florence & Tuscany
Florida
France
Germany
Greek Islands
Hawai'i
India
Ireland
Israel
Italy
Japan
London
Mexico
Moscow &
St. Petersburg
New York City
Paris
Portugal
Prague
Provence
Rome
San Francisco
Scotland
Singapore & Malaysia
South Africa
Spain
Thailand
Turkey
Venice
Vietnam

Flashmaps
Boston
New York
San Francisco
Washington, D.C.

Fodor's Cityguides
Boston
New York
San Francisco

Fodor's Gay Guides
Amsterdam
Los Angeles &
Southern California

New York City
Pacific Northwest
San Francisco and
the Bay Area
South Florida
USA

Karen Brown Guides
Austria
California
England B&Bs
England, Wales &
Scotland
France B&Bs
France Inns
Germany
Ireland
Italy B&Bs
Italy Inns
Portugal
Spain
Switzerland

Languages for Travelers (Cassette & Phrasebook)
French
German
Italian
Spanish

Mobil Travel Guides
America's Best
Hotels & Restaurants
Arizona
California and the
West
Florida
Great Lakes
Major Cities
Mid-Atlantic
Northeast
Northwest and
Great Plains
Southeast
Southern California
Southwest and
South Central

Pocket Guides
Acapulco
Aruba
Atlanta
Barbados
Beijing
Berlin
Budapest
Dublin
Honolulu
Jamaica
London
Mexico City
New York City
Paris

Prague
Puerto Rico
Rome
San Francisco
Savannah &
Charleston
Shanghai
Sydney
Washington, D.C.

Rivages Guides
Bed and Breakfasts of
Character and Charm
in France
Hotels and Country
Inns of Character and
Charm in France
Hotels and Country
Inns of Character and
Charm in Italy
Hotels and Country
Inns of Character and
Charm in Paris
Hotels and Country
Inns of Character and
Charm in Portugal
Hotels and Country
Inns of Character and
Charm in Spain
Wines & Vineyards
of Character and
Charm in France

Short Escapes
Britain
France
Near New York City
New England

Fodor's Sports
Golf Digest's
Places to Play (USA)
Golf Digest's Places to
Play in the Southeast
Golf Digest's Places to
Play in the Southwest
Skiing USA
USA Today The
Complete Four Sport
Stadium Guide

Fodor's upCLOSE Guides
California
Europe
France
Great Britain
Ireland
Italy
London
Los Angeles
Mexico
New York City
Paris
San Francisco

WHEREVER YOU TRAVEL, *H*ELP IS NEVER FAR AWAY.

From planning your trip to

providing travel assistance along

the way, American Express®

Travel Service Offices are

always there to help

you do more.